DEGENERATION IN THE GREAT FRENCH MASTERS

DEGENERATION IN THE GREAT FRENCH MASTERS

ROUSSEAU — CHATEAUBRIAND — BALZAC
— STENDHAL — SAND — MUSSET — BAUDE-
LAIRE — FLAUBERT — VERLAINE — ZOLA

By JEAN CARRÈRE

TRANSLATED BY JOSEPH McCABE

Essay Index Reprint Series

BOOKS FOR LIBRARIES PRESS, INC.
FREEPORT, NEW YORK

First Published 1922
Reprinted 1967

LIBRARY OF CONGRESS CATALOG CARD NUMBER: 67-26722

PRINTED IN THE UNITED STATES OF AMERICA

PREFATORY NOTE

FEW readers will go far in these brilliant and stimulating pages without asking: "Who is Jean Carrère?" He is a master of French prose in its purest limpidity, a poet of fine inspiration and rich imagery, a profound student of human nature and of all literature, a prophet of lofty ideals, yet the most patient and indulgent of critics. In other words, he represents a rare combination of the qualities of the literary critic, the journalist, the poet, the moralist, and the humanist; and there could be no more excellent equipment for the work, which he accomplishes in this forceful and elegant little volume, of disentangling unhealthy sentiment from exquisite art and charm of personality in the great writers of modern France.

M. Carrère was well known in England twenty-two years ago, when he was quite a young man. He was a French war correspondent with the British Army in South Africa. He criticised us—Heaven knows there was much to criticise!—but he made France understand us. "At last there is somebody in France who understands us," said the *Daily Graphic* at the time. His vivid, picturesque, intensely humane articles were quoted everywhere. And the outcome of it all gave him a task. He interpreted England and France to each other; and from the rancorous and acrid mutual misconceptions of 1900 we passed quickly to the Entente.

Carrère went on to render the same service to France and Italy. He is profoundly, devotedly Latin; for he is above all things classical, an admirer and pupil of the serene type of greatness in Homer and Vergil. So again the poet and man of letters anonymously helped to shape and guide the world-process. M. Carrère is a modest man, and it is necessary to give these details in explanation of the vague references he makes in these pages to his work and his travels.

Behind it all, from the start, was a larger ideal. He had ventured upon the sea of letters, from the Latin Quarter at Paris, in the early nineties. He says, in this book, that he began with all the artistic irresponsibility of the prevailing school. But do not take him too literally. By 1897 he was writing such verse as

> Let us flee idle dreams and that sadness impure,

and

> For the poem is a cry in the battles of men.

He was for manliness, health, struggle, joyous labour, strong sunlight, serenity, law. He very early took up the work of Mistral. He had been called the *roi des Écoles*, the king of 4,000 students, in 1893. His influence grew, and from the end of the nineteenth century he used it on behalf of what he calls always the *solar* ideal of life. The youth of France was obsessed by poetry which commended life in the light of the moon: soft, dim, evasive, querulous, dreamy. And France seemed to be decaying.

That is the keynote of these essays. That is why they begin with Rousseau, and include the Catholic Chateaubriand. M. Carrère is one of the least sectarian of men, and one of the most human. His point of view is original precisely because it is so broadly human. He pleads only for manliness (*vir-tus*). But his pleading and his censuring are supported by so impartial and discriminating a sentiment—so much of the " serenity " he urges—so acute a knowledge of human nature, and so high an artistic quality, that he is as captivating as he is original.

It remains only to extenuate a little boldness on the part of the translator. These essays necessarily quote some of the finest verse of modern France. Where the poems have already been translated, the work of these more leisurely and more qualified translators of poetry has been used. But much remained; and this version is essentially for the man who does not read French. I decided, therefore, to render the lines into an English which should show both the structure of the verse and the exact sentiments of the poets—which the familiar translations rarely do—and the lapse from æsthetic grace must be pardoned.

The French title, *Les Mauvais Maîtres* (*The Bad Masters*), would mislead an English public, unaccustomed to French subtlety. I have changed it. But it must be borne in mind throughout the reading of the work.

J. M.

Dedication

TO

MY FRIEND ANTOINE ALBALAT

*Y*OU *have often asked me for this book. So much the worse for you, therefore, if I put your name at the head of it. Perhaps you remember its stormy adventures when, from 1902 to 1904, it appeared, in weekly instalments, in the* Revue Hebdomadaire. *Thanks to the large circulation of that well-known periodical, which was good enough to present these pages, they made some stir in the small world of letters. The mildest charge brought against me was that it was unpatriotic to depreciate in this shameless fashion, in the eyes of foreigners who read the review, so many glorious representatives of the French race. In regard to Rousseau, in particular, one newspaper said that I had insulted Switzerland, in recalling that Jean Jacques was born at Geneva. Another said that, in praising the work of Dante to the detriment of that of Rousseau, I had put monarchic imperialism above the spirit of the Revolution.*

But it was the pages devoted to George Sand and Musset which brought upon me the most eloquent maledictions. Young men of the time—now, doubtless, austere heads of families—wrote that, since I uttered such blasphemies against the divinity of love, I must be a sour and sombre misogynist to whom Heaven had refused all the rapturous inebriations of heart and sense. As to my studies of Balzac, Stendhal, Baudelaire, Flaubert, and Verlaine, they, unhappily, drew upon me the awful sentence of major excommunication from the reviews which decree the lot of

*poets ; I was sternly banished from the republic of letters,
without the compensation of the Platonist wreath of flowers.*

*I bore all these anathemas in silence. I even intended,
without malice, to make a single volume of these closely
related essays, when the accidents of a busy life took me
away from my country, and compelled me to yield to the
insidious attraction of a political and international activity
in which I was absorbed for more than ten years. Then
everybody became wrapped up in the War, and so for more
than fifteen years these studies have been buried at the bottom
of my papers. It seems that in the meantime some of the
ideas stated briefly in my notes in the* Revue Hebdomadaire
*were taken up by distinguished colleagues, and were given
to the public in sonorous lectures which were discussed for
a year or two. What luck for my ideas! It is even said that
the title of my essays was borrowed by over-enthusiastic
admirers. What good fortune for the title! The only
thing I regret is that they did not take my title and my articles
bodily, and publish them in full over some well-known
literary signature. That would have spared me the trouble
of finding a publisher ; a formality for which I have always
had little inclination. It affords me real pleasure to cast
my living words into the stormy sea of journals and reviews,
which are active and dynamic elements ; but I have small
disposition to bury them, in a calf binding, in the vaults
of our libraries. If there were no restless friends and
relatives urging me to bring together occasionally a few pages
of prose or verse, it would be my supreme joy to leave all my
works posthumous. How much trouble one would escape
by doing that! The works themselves, moreover, would
lose nothing. If they are immortal, why be in a hurry?
And if they are not immortal, why publish them at all ?*

*But our friends are terribly exacting. They are deter-
mined at any price to make us famous. They know no rest
until they have hurled us, palpitating, into the open jaws
of the public. I never meet an old friend but he asks :*

"What about your writing? Have you quite given it up ?"

Dedication

"*What about your poetry? Have you done with it?*"

"*What about those essays? Are you never going to publish them?*"

Sometimes, to escape their ironical persistence, I untruthfully announced that I would publish a book in the coming spring, and thus, by repeated postponements, I gained a few pleasant years of literary obscurity; which is the only state wherein true lovers of glory can live happily. But it is no longer possible to find excuses. The long struggle to which I was devoted abroad has, for good or evil, come to a close. The War seems to be over. Art flourishes again, apparently, on every side. People turn with the old passion to the enjoyment of letters. If I would have peace, I am compelled to publish a few works; and I begin with these irrepressible essays, mercilessly dedicating them to you.

Yet, believe me, I remain your friend,

J. C.

ROME,
March, 1921.

FOREWORD

I APPROACH a task which requires a courage, and is beset by dangers, of which I cannot be ignorant. It is to ascertain which of the great poets and writers of the last century a thoughtful observer may justly blame for that state of intellectual disturbance, of moral listlessness, of public unrest, in which so many of our young men seem to find at once a source of pleasure and a ground of lament.

And the first objection that will be raised is that one invests literature with an exaggerated importance when one casts the responsibility for this situation upon the men who make books. To that I reply, simply, that from the dawn of historical time until our own day books have been the sole means of preserving and transmitting the moral treasures of the race. All that we know about past ages has been learned from the men who wrote in them. All education is but a commentary upon written works. Civilisation and literature are indispensable to each other. Without letters, indeed, our life would tend to be a ceaseless repetition of the same experiences and the same blunders; we could not compare our age with its predecessors.

The soul which animates us to-day was moulded by the poets, the historians, the thinkers whose voices come to us out of the tomb of the last six thousand years; and something of what we write to-day will pass into the soul of generations to come. We should, were we fully conscious of our power to cloud or to illumine the mind of the advancing race, almost tremble with emotion whenever we publish a new page.

Not all classes of books have equal influence, however; and, of all the forms in which the thought of man may clothe itself, the best and the worst, the most terrible and the most beneficent, is the form presented to us in works of imagination—" poetry."

To works of argument or learning, books that proclaim or assail ideas, whether in history, philosophy, morals, or religion, there is a counteracting force in other works. The evil of one book is undone by the good of others. Let an historian publish a work that breathes hatred of some nation, some king, some hero. Forthwith there comes another with a defence or an apology; and then, perhaps, a third who puts the facts impartially. It is the same with philosophy and morals. Where Heraclitus affirms, Democritus denies. When one thinker recommends inaction and indifference, another fires us with the need of will and energy. We remain masters of ourselves. We can accept or reject their ideas.

Not so with the poet. He is the supreme master in his own domain. In the strict etymological sense the poet (from *poiein*, to create) is he who derives from his own genius a whole world of facts, emotions, and images, and breathes into them the throbbing vitality of real existence. He is the novelist as well as the lyricist, the dramatist and the musician, the inventor of fables and the inventor of epics.

It is precisely in virtue of this power to create an independent world that the poet is either magnificent or terrible. He does not argue; he does not prove things. He invents. He does not convince us: he seduces us. He passes into our being; as do fair scenes, the murmurs of the forest, the mirrorings of the calm sea, the freshness of the night, the splendour of the sun. He conquers us; we are powerless to defend ourselves. Only if he be tiresome, mediocre, can he leave us unmoved; but in that case he does not exist. Grant him genius, and he is irresistible. He forces upon us the perfume of his flowers, the tranquil shade of his forests, the lines of his horizon; and we strive in vain to elude his magical power. We are prisoners of his charm. What can we do to rid ourselves of the pictures he has created in us ? Shall we go to another poet ? One does not refute an epic by an epic, a drama by a drama, an ode by a sonnet. That is the root of all the good and all the evil a poet may do. He can plant in us either the seed of heroism or the germ of cowardice. He is a " master."

There are good masters and bad masters. The responsibility, the mission, of the poet I do not propose to ascertain and define here. Ever since the *quique pii vates* of Vergil, the Demodocos of Homer, singing before Ulysses in the gardens of Alcinous, the chorus of Æschylus and the cosmogony of Orpheus, the poet's mission has been unalterably defined. The good poet, the beneficent master, is the builder of cities, the creator of heroes, the inspirer of energy, the giver of light, the sun-like radiant being.

Every great poet is heroic. By that quality we measure his greatness. There is something more than a secret affinity between the hero and the poet; there is a vital connection. The one sustains the other, and is sustained by him. They are two flowers from one sap; both are born of the same yearning of mankind for an ideal nobleness. Almost always there is a poet in the hero, and a hero in the true poet. For both of them life and work are an eternal self-dedication to the bettering of the race. Bestowal of oneself, love of one's fellows, deep

pity, disdain of material enjoyments, suffering borne to
make the future glorious—these are the common features
of hero and poet. We need not brood over the lives of
the poets; we need not summon the shades of such
splendid heroes of action as Orpheus, Æschylus, Sophocles,
Dante, Cervantes, and Lamartine. We need only glance
at their works to realise what strength we draw from
the beneficent masters. All great, virile, robust poets
have breathed into us the love of life, depicted for us the
victory of will over passion, spurred us to make glorious
sacrifices—have, in a word, roused us to *heroism*. In
two magnificent strophes of Mistral you have the most
perfect of poetic arts:

> Pour out the poet's wine,
>   Singing of man and God;
> For 'tis the food divine
>   That lifts the human clod.
>
> Pour out the wit to know
>   Things good and true and brave,
> And every joy bestow
>   That laughs e'en at the grave.

Whatever their land, their race, their religion, their
philosophy, we recognise " good masters " by the strength
which they give. We have Homer and his Ulysses,
Æschylus and his Prometheus, Sophocles and his Antigone, Vergil and his Æneas; we have Dante, Rabelais,*
Calderon, Milton, Shakespeare, Corneille, Goethe, Lamartine, Vigny, Hugo, Ibsen, Tolstoi, Wagner. And how far
from complete the list is! The whole of the higher
classical literature is, in all its forms, one vast triumph
of the male spirit—luminous, balanced, harmonious—
over the female spirit—nocturnal, disturbed, unhealthy.
In every great poet there must be, as there is in Orpheus,

* See Note 1 (at end of volume).

an apostle of the sun. Not without reason did the Greeks make Apollo the god of the muses.

But there are, as I said, bad as well as beneficent masters. It need not be explained that we are not here concerned about literary and artistic quality, about the *ability* of writers. A poet who has no invention, no style, no genius, does not count. He may have an ephemeral success, but he has no lasting fame and no influence. Upon him we will not waste our time.

By a " bad master," a source of degeneration, I mean one who, gifted with the power to seduce men by the charm and wealth of his imagination, by his skill in weaving harmonious and captivating phrases, instead of urging himself toward heroism and drawing toward it the souls which he influences, surrenders himself in his writings to all the weaknesses of passion and all the seductions of the life of ease, uses his talent for the exaltation of mean pleasures and gross desires, and on that account becomes, for those whom he has enchanted, a teacher of weakness, egoism, cowardice, and cupidity. The good master is the one who leads us toward an ideal of strength and light: the bad master is the one who leaves us with mind overcast and senses quivering.

There have been in all literatures bad masters of this character. Some, men and women of incomparable grace and ability, count amongst the immortals. In Greece there were Anacreon, Sappho, Euripides, and Lucian; at Rome, Tibullus, Catullus, even Horace, Ovid, Suetonius, and Petronius; in France the greatest of them were Villon, Montaigne, and Jean Jacques Rousseau. But the last century was the chief period of their reign. In that epoch of general confusion and disturbance of the nations, all sorts of larvæ emerged from the depths of human nature, and bad masters arose on every side;

masters of souls more effectively than ever before, yet beyond question bad. Too weak to resist the degeneration that environed them, they were, nevertheless, strong enough to create enduring work. On that account their influence was especially mischievous, and it persists to-day. It has fallen so surely upon all of us that one has only to point to it to raise angry protests.

These bad masters still enjoy their victory. They have ardent, loyal, all-powerful defenders. That is why I cannot hesitate to enter the lists against them.

CONTENTS

xix

JEAN JACQUES ROUSSEAU

Few men have mourned as I have mourned: few have shed
so many tears in the course of their lives.—*Confessions*, I. iii.

DEGENERATION IN THE GREAT FRENCH MASTERS

CHAPTER I

JEAN JACQUES ROUSSEAU

I

Know ye the heavenly seed from which ye came.
Not for the lusts of beast were ye compacted,
But that your minds and hearts be set aflame.

THESE verses of the most superb of the Western poets, these lines of Dante, of which every robust and sonorous word seems to impart strength, come irresistibly to my memory whenever I think of Jean Jacques Rousseau.

This is, in the first place, because the words of the wonderful Florentine—words taken from the most virile and most sunny of all languages—are precisely the contrary of the famous apostrophe in which Jean Jacques gives us a synthesis of his dark and feeble spirit:

All-powerful God, who dost hold all spirits in Thy hands, free us from the light and the pernicious art of our fathers, and restore to us ignorance, innocence, and poverty, which alone can make us happy, and are precious in Thy sight.

But I recall the words also because between Dante and Rousseau there is something else besides the contrast of two very different characters and two entirely opposite literary conceptions. When you regard them carefully, they seem to approach each other, in virtue of that very contrast between two formidable and almost uncontrollable natures which they present. This approximation

23

at once gives us an unexpected light in which we see new features of each towering genius.

Both of them, prodigies as they are, issue from the conflicts of ideas which stirred the world at the time they were on earth. Both of them are so thoroughly original, such obvious innovators, that one cannot possibly connect their work with that of any writer who preceded them. Both of them inaugurate a literature, and enrich it with new figures of speech, brilliant visions, bold and expressive terms, new impulses of lyrical aspiration, striking personifications. Such is the personal ardour of each that one would almost say that they create themselves the vigorous and sonorous speech in which their thoughts are so splendidly clothed. Yet both, in spite of the difference of education, have in such measure the gift of selecting the proper and harmonious word that their style brings them indisputably into the company of the world's great writers. The verse of Dante recalls to us that of Homer and Vergil: the prose of Rousseau reminds us of the ample periods of Demosthenes, Livy, Cicero, and Bossuet.

It is not merely the similarity of their powers, but still more the analogy of their mission, which urges both of them into the storm of public life. Neither of them was a tranquil and comfortable man of letters, giving a leisurely polish to some delectable work. They are, both of them, stirrers of souls, rousers of humanity. They cannot write a single verse, a single line, that is not the vibrant echo of the conflict of their age, and that will not in its turn re-echo in the conflicts of the future. Moreover, almost identical sufferings and adventures give fire and passion to the mind and heart of each.

Both of them are at war with the age in which they live. Both of them wander over Europe with little security of life. Both of them know the bitterness of having to appeal to others. And—to complete this strange relationship—both of them seek in vain some hour of serene and peaceful speech as the stormy life draws to a close; and both of them, sustaining to the end the hatred of their fellows, die in exile or in despair. Then, the moment they are dead, both of them are raised as high as the clouds by the praise of men, those amongst whom they had suffered almost making gods of them.

From destinies so curiously similar one would expect works of much the same inspiration. One would be disposed to find Dante and Rousseau, like Horace and Vergil, Sophocles and Racine, Menander and Molière, Petrarch and Goethe, and so many others of different tongues and lands, and even of markedly different personalities, a pair of brothers in genius, such as arise at all points of time and space to show the identity in succeeding civilisations, the persistence of an equilibrium in the productions of the human mind amidst all the seeming annihilations of ideas and literatures.

II

We do not. In spite of the similarity of their circumstances, in spite of the astonishing affinities of their gifts, there could be no more striking contradiction than that which we find between the work of Dante and the work of Rousseau. They seem, like hostile brothers whom everything tends to alienate, to have sought the very antipodes of the world of thought and sentiment. They are so far from each other, so drastically opposed to each other, that it almost seems strange that one should dare to compare them. Yet they are like and unlike each other as are two aspects of the same scene, when one sees it in succession under the blaze of the sun and in the darkness of dusk. In a sense they illumine each other; or, rather, the one which is in the light brings out the real contour and details of the one who remains in the shade. When we study them together, we appreciate better the luminous power of the one and the dark strength of the other.

It looks as if nature and history, both lovers of antithesis, have conspired to produce in almost the same circumstances, separated by five centuries of time, two beings to whom they have granted the same gifts of intelligence and utterance, the same power of influencing and moving, and—an excessive love of experiment—the same stormy career. But to one they gave the heart of a hero, to the other the heart of a coward.

There you have the fundamental difference between them in work and influence. In Dante we have a mind passionate but lucid, profoundly moved but far-seeing, of vast vision, a creator of beauty and energy, an elixir of strength, a tonic for the feeble. In Rousseau we see the unsteady development of a mind at once confused, nervous, and ardent; a mind that boldly assails impossibilities, yet halts timidly before quite simple possibilities; crushed by the past, terrified by the present, alarmed at the future; spreading around it all the symptoms of terror and impotence which it itself exhibits.

The one, in spite of his passion, his anger, even his injustice, has so radiant and purifying a flame in his soul, breathes so helpful a strength from his work, that one feels better when one approaches him. Whole nations have found courage and restoration in the cult of him.

The other, in spite of his thirst for an ideal justice, in spite of his dreams of goodness and his ardent desire to serve his fellows, leaves such trouble in our minds and such weakness in our hearts that, in his company, we find ourselves rather ashamed of being human. Through him one learns all the stains and failures of human nature, and one feels, after reading his works, smaller, weaker, irresolute, incapable of effort, eager for the repose of non-existence, stirred only with hatred of life.

Dante, in a word, is a virile and sunny genius, not, perhaps, the most perfect, but the most robust of the beneficent masters. Rousseau is, on the contrary, a feminine genius, a genius of the night. He is all uncertainty and weakness. He is, by the very force of his genius and his indisputable originality, the most mischievous and most influential of the bad masters.

None could venture to contradict us when we say that Rousseau was one of the greatest geniuses whose word ever stirred the world; that his work is grandiose and astounding; that his style has an incomparable novelty and beauty; that he extorts our admiration, even our sympathy, by the smooth and large flow of his eloquence and the sincerity of his fiery passion; that, in a word, he was a great writer and a great man. How is it, then, that this great man and great writer does not inspire us with light and strength, but leaves us in confusion and irresolution? How is it that we are all compelled to admit that we feel ourselves less good at heart and less clear in mind after reading the author of the *Confessions* and *Émile*, whereas we always find ourselves stronger after reading the *Divine Comedy*? How is it that the very passions, invectives, even hatreds of the exiled Florentine glow with splendour and endow us with strength, while the passions, invectives, and hatreds of the wandering son of Geneva leave us troubled, unbalanced, and morally enfeebled?

That is a point to be studied closely if we would understand Rousseau's work and detect its fundamental vice; and we shall discover it by means of an illuminating comparison. We shall find that Dante is the moral guide of nations and of poets because he always sacrificed his humble personality in a public cause, and that Rousseau is a source of disorder and impotence because he was always ready to sacrifice order and the public cause to his own overweening personality.

III

I know that in using this language I am apt to shock many of my contemporaries. I am the better prepared to expect their astonishment and annoyance as I long shared their error, and I regard it still with a certain sympathy. But it is important to make my position clear at the very outset of these studies and to open a direct attack upon the real evil, which is individualism.

Those sacred rights of the individual! Did I not once accept with my whole soul—did I not devote my youth to defending—this free development of personality, these proud and frenzied claims which the apostles of " self," from Rousseau to Ibsen and Nietzsche, have hurled at us? And how little it moves me that others defend them to-day! Unlike the converts who pass from sect to sect, I have a particular affection for those who cherish the illusions which once appealed to myself.

Shall I tell what personal and public experiences swept away the clouds in which my individualist chimera was enthroned, and let me see it clearly? For that I should need to tell the long story of my life and travels, and few would be interested. All that I need say is that, as I passed through various countries and studied different

28

civilisations, as I resolutely tore myself away from
books and flung myself into the conflicts of life and the
turmoil of antagonistic passions, I one day saw with entire
clearness, almost as if it had a material reality, this truth
of reason and experience, that the individual, however
great he may be, is but a single wave on the surface of
the sea, a single blade of grass on the broad plain; that he
is, of himself, an incoherent and feeble animal, the feeblest
and most defenceless of all. All that he can do, all that
he has, all that he knows, all that he has won from nature
—rather, all that has been won for him—he owes to the
mysterious, perhaps divine, instinct which has for ages
impelled men to gather in harmonious groups, to form
associations, under a reasonable and progressive contract,
in order to meet the forces which threaten them, to
emerge from the disorder of natural life and develop in
the protective order of social life. All that men are,
from the new-born babe which finds its clothes and
cradle prepared for it to emperors and popes upon their
thrones, is due to the continuous and multiplied efforts
of millions of individuals whose obscure and laborious
lives have filled the ages; all is due to *society*. I am but
a single link lost in the vast network of millions of chains
that stretches over time and space. I am attached to
the whole of history; I am one with the whole of humanity.
And if, by some violent effort of imagination, I try to strip
myself of all that society has wrapped about me, I sink
to the level of the sordid beast, the obscene ape, the lost
dog. I return to savagery. Well, I have seen savages.
I have seen them as close to nature as they can be seen
in our days. I have not studied their ways in books or
in exhibitions. I have been in their huts, have smelt
their dung-heaps. . . . No, thank you. Since that time
I have fully understood how much I owe to the labour,

during thousands of years, of those who have gone before me.

Where is, in nature, the right of the individual ? His one natural right is to wander naked through the forests, to fight wild beasts, to eat whatever food he can wrest from the rival appetite of his fellows, free and savage like himself. All other rights—absolutely all—a man owes to society.

And if some day this society, rightly or wrongly, refuses me something, and I demand its destruction, am I not rather like a character in a comedy ? It is the impulsive anger of a savage, or, rather, the amusing gesture of a selfish and angry child. At least let us, in such case, restore to society all that it has given us. Let us take nothing, good or evil, from it. Let us strip ourselves of all that we owe to it, and, as Voltaire said to Rousseau, " let us live on all fours."

IV

But to say, as is often said, that Rousseau was an " egoist " is to give an incomplete and crude description of him. Precise as it is in its literal signification, the word is so vague and ambiguous in its various applications that it does not help us in the least to understand the prodigious genius and the nefarious influence of the great writer. Indeed, if we take it strictly, it cannot justly be used in connection with Jean Jacques.

If, by " egoist " we mean the kind of indifferent and gross being whom La Bruyère depicts so well, the being who knows nothing of a surrounding world except as a possible source of pleasure to himself, Jean Jacques Rousseau was not an egoist. A genuine, thorough egoist in the popular meaning of the word, and with the features sketched for us by the author of *Characters*, would be quite unable to create any work whatever, or to interest himself in any work. He would have neither the sympathy nor the indignation, neither the deep sense of pain nor the great anger; not even a real passion. He would gluttonously seize all the pleasures within his reach, and he would resolutely avoid the trouble of thinking. Such a being exists in great numbers. He lives all round us, in millions of specimens which are incessantly renewed. He never does any good. Sometimes he does no great harm; or, at least, the harm he does is limited to his own narrow range. He lives, or vegetates, at the lowest stage of material humanity. He has nothing in common with Rousseau, whose soul had sublime flights, whose heart beat with tenderness, who seethed with impulsive passion; who, above all others, gave himself to every man who approached him, and burned with a desire to see the whole human race happy, virtuous, and just.

Not only was Jean Jacques not indifferent to the spectacle of life about him, but he was aroused by the faintest cry; he suffered at every glimpse of misery; he revolted against injustice and pain. Can anyone say that he thought only of himself when, throughout his life, he was unhappy precisely because he loved, without stint or measure, all who crossed his path ?—when, in the strength of some passionate disillusion, he did not hate and curse them. Love and hatred are, by their very ardour, their power of expansion, the exact antithesis of the indifferent and gross egoism which is the radical vice of so many obscure souls.

If, on the other hand, one takes the word " egoist " in the high and philosophic sense in which it is applied to men of great ambition, to those who handle men or money on a large scale, those whose absorbing and devouring activity seeks to bring under their increasing control all that come within their orbit, it is still inapplicable to Jean Jacques Rousseau. Certainly he never had the ruthless passion of the master of men; one might, indeed, justly reproach him with the opposite vice. He had, perhaps, the ambition to win glory, but not the lust of direct power. On a lower plane, he had no ambition for money or honours. Indeed, in spite of his incredible mendicity, in spite of the ugly things of which he accuses himself, we must say that he was really disinterested. Not without a certain nobility he could write:

No, No. I say, with equal truth and pride, that never, at any period of my life, did either interest or indigence move my heart to act or refrain from acting. Throughout the course of an uneven life, a life memorable for its hard fortunes, often without shelter and without bread, I have ever kept an impartial eye upon wealth and misery. . . . Never has poverty, or the dread of it, wrung from me a single sigh or a single tear. In all my trials my soul has recognised only the good and the evil that depend upon it; and it was when I lacked nothing that was necessary that I felt myself the most miserable of mortals.

The whole of this eloquent passage is true, even to the sombre avowal of the last line, in which there appears what we shall find to be the real defect of Rousseau.

Jean Jacques was neither indifferent to the sufferings of others nor incapable of attachment and friendship, neither covetous, nor greedy, nor so much as interested in this world's goods. We must therefore admit that he was no egoist, either in the gross fashion of the more servile animals or in the proud and voracious way of lions and vultures.

V

Would it be correct, as a description of Rousseau's work or an indication of its general spirit, to say that he was an *individualist* ?

It is true, as we shall see at the close of this study, that the powerful influence of Jean Jacques initiated in the poetry of the nineteenth century a current of unhealthy individualism, of which Chateaubriand, Musset, George Sand, Flaubert, Stendhal, and Baudelaire were the most famous and most characteristic issues. It is true that all Rousseau's works of fiction, and even most of his philosophical works, end in an exaltation of the individual. It is, in fact, indisputable that the author of the *Discourse on the Origin and Foundations of Inequality amongst Men* was the first in the history of letters and philosophy to formulate, clearly and precisely, the eminently anti-social, anti-human, and even anti-historical principle, that the individual is born good, free, and happy, and is perverted, dominated, and thwarted by society, of which he is the victim. Rousseau was the first seriously and dogmatically to deny the need of civilisation and preach the return to nature. There is, therefore, no lack of evidence for those who make the author of *Émile* the theorist and apostle of political and moral individualism.

Yet he was not. He was no more an individualist than he was an egoist; or, rather, if he became an individualist, and must be counted such in his posthumous influence on account of the consequences of his work, it was in spite of himself and contrary to his express design—it was from weakness, not from will.

The genuine individualist disdains, despises, or hates humanity, or he is at least indifferent to its successive transformations. He feels no impulse either to correct or to destroy it. He affects to be alien, useless, and superior to it. He takes all that he can from it, and gives it as little as he can; and he creates for himself in the midst of it a sort of stronghold in which he lives for himself, glancing at men from the summits of his towers. He

C

does not, like those giant egoists whose ambition disturbs and torments everyone within range, want to be the centre of the world. No, he is himself the world: the only world in which he takes any interest. He notices the affairs of men only in so far as they may serve or hurt himself.

The real prototype of the individualist is the listless, disdainful, aristocratic Montaigne; at a later date it is the melancholic, indolent, haughty Chateaubriand. Neither of them wishes to see any change of the established order of things. The one smiles at it from his placid retreat; the other experiences it in his sterile agitation. Both of them know that all effort is useless, except the exertion which procures some pleasure or, at times, some pain—which is the pleasure of certain souls.

Rousseau has nothing in common with this supreme indifference to social life. On the contrary, he is eaten up with the zeal of an apostle and reformer. He burns to transform society. If at times he lashes it with invective and furiously assails it, this is because he dreams of transforming it to the shape of his own ideal. He has the proselytic spirit pushed to the degree of monomania. He wants all men to think and to live as he does; he wants them all to attain happiness by the same means which he would himself employ. When he wants to bring back the whole race to the life of nature, it is for the good of the race. So far from despising his fellows, or being indifferent to their troubles, he is devoured by an eloquent, if impotent, ardour to obtain for them those chimerical joys which his never-resting imagination fabricates.

It would, therefore, be equally unjust and absurd to charge the author of the *Social Contract* with individualism. He is, on the contrary, a zealous " altruist " (to use a modern barbarism). He hates society only out of love of men. He becomes misanthropic through the excesses of his philanthropy.

He is, in reality, neither an egoist nor an individualist; yet he acts and speaks like an egoist, and he bequeaths to the world a vast and powerful work which will infallibly, in the next century, lead to the exaltation of individual passions to the detriment of social needs. That is the paradox of Jean Jacques Rousseau.

What is the cause of this divergence of intention and realisation ? How is it that a man who would be good and virtuous becomes pernicious in his influence and cowardly in his life ?

It is because he was more deeply tainted than any other by a malady which fell upon many souls in the latter part of the eighteenth, and during the whole course of the nineteenth, century: the malady of " self," a dark and distressing preoccupation with one's own personality. Rousseau was certainly neither an egoist nor an individualist, but he was what we may call an " egomaniac."

This kind of " egomania " is not inconsistent with a desire to be good and with feelings of affection for one's fellows. But the egomaniac is convinced that the whole race is interested in his joys and sorrows. His pain and pleasure are universal pains and pleasures. He does not understand the reason of his sufferings nor, consequently, of the sufferings of others. He dreams that he has a great destiny; and he imagines one for the entire planet. He draws a picture of himself; and he judges the rest of men by this picture, in which he takes great pleasure.

" I am good," says this sick man, " and my fellows seem to me wicked. Either society is wrong, then, or I am an exception produced by nature. So let us change society, and reveal to it, in its new form, such a man as I am."

The whole work of Rousseau rests upon this double illusion. He was not, in spite of his own words, an exception in the race, especially in his age. This malady attacks men at times of excessive civilisation, when the visible order seems to leave no room for personal initiative, and some strong traditional discipline seems to have settled for ever the fixed balance of social relations. In such cases many evils remain hidden and inevitable, as they do beneath the external splendour of all social order. Men with generous instincts are born, and they see the evils and burn to heal them. They find themselves powerless, and, falling back upon themselves, their imagination is aflame with all that they wished to do, and could not. If, like Goethe, they are strong, they, in the torture of their youth, raise a cry of revolt against life, and dream of an impassioned suicide. Then they are healed, and their growing virility restores the balance which a juvenile and suppressed ardour had disturbed. But if they are weak, devoid of energy, of irresolute will, voluptuous, feminine, cowardly at heart, they become more and more obsessed with their selves as they advance in life, and the harm is increased when they see so many evils born of a society for which they know no reason. They regard themselves as the incarnation of human sorrow. They believe that they are encompassed by a universal hatred, and that society is furiously bent upon persecuting them, solely because they are superior to other men. If they have eloquence and genius, they declare war upon this stepmotherly, this ridiculous, society; and they magnify their own overweening and hypersensitive personalities.

Thus it is that Rousseau comes to write:

I have conceived an enterprise which is without precedent, and which, when it is carried out, will never be imitated. I will

show my fellows a man in the whole truth of nature, and this
man shall be myself.

I alone ! I read my heart, and I know men. I am not made
like any of the men I have seen: I venture to think that I am not
made like other any man in the world. I may be no better, but
I am at all events different. Whether nature did well or ill to
break the mould in which she cast me cannot be decided until
my book has been read.

These are the words of a fool, some are sure to say.
No, this is no fool. It is simply the illusion of a man who
thinks that the whole of nature, the whole earth, everything, even the fruits of a slow social evolution, were made
solely for him.

We all know this man : we all *are* this man in some degree
or other. And so when, in the decline of a civilisation,
there appears a great poet who, magnificently and in
resounding tones, embodies and utters this morbid, but
universal, frame of mind, he gains a formidable influence
over the souls of men. Unconsciously egoistic, he becomes
the guide of all unconscious egoists. Panegyrist of pride,
he awakens sonorous echoes in the vain depths of our
darkened souls.

VI

Rousseau glorified all the troubles and passions of a
moribund world, while Dante extolled all the heroisms
of a world that struggled for birth. Similar in their
genius, they brought entirely different souls to the task;
and each proved capable of incarnating the confused
aspirations of his time. Dante was vigorous, energetic,
lucid, brave in pain, strong in misfortune; Rousseau was
feeble, without energy, without courage, without will.
Dante, staggering under a burden of evil, never makes a
personal complaint. When he trembles with anger,

he is contemplating the miseries of his country and his age:

Ah ! serva Italia, di dolore ostello !

Rousseau, on the contrary, even in his periods of material peace thinks only of his own griefs, of the sufferings of his sensitive soul.

Few men have mourned as I have mourned: few have shed so many tears in the course of their lives.

He makes for himself a kind of aureole of his suffering; he does not see that suffering borne thus, without resistance, without courage, without effort to remove it, is a degradation of soul, a lowering of personality. He broods over his pain because it is an enjoyment. Somewhere he speaks rapturously of " that sensitiveness of heart which makes us find joy in ourselves."

In brief, Rousseau is a voluptuary, a man of passion. He finds more charm in weeping than in struggling. He is the nerveless soldier who halts by the way, throws down his arms, and buries his forehead in his hands. He says:

Apart from the one object which I pursue the universe is nothing to me. But all that lasts only a moment; the next moment plunges me into annihilation.

This feeble, lachrymose, gloomy soul has multiplied itself by the glamour and influence of the *Confessions*, *Émile*, the *Nouvelle Héloise*, and the eloquent *Discours*. It created a whole new literature; and the prestige of this literature still dazes us. Rousseau was the father of morbid Romanticism; Dante the spirit which evoked the luminous Renaissance and the glorious classical centuries. We shall meet again this malady of " self," in different forms, in all the " bad masters " of the nineteenth century. It will inspire the melancholy of Chateaubriand, the vulgar ambition of Balzac's heroes, the misanthropy of Stendhal, the rebellious passion of George Sand, Flaubert's despair, the amorous feebleness of Musset, Baudelaire's dream, Verlaine's moral decadence, and Zola's pessimism. There is in the work of Rousseau the germ of all that is unhealthy in the nineteenth century.

FRANÇOIS RENÉ DE CHATEAUBRIAND

Who, in the early years of the nineteenth century, led astray the soul of France ? Probably it was, above all others, Chateaubriand.—REMY DE GOURMONT : *La Sensibilité romantique.* See Note 2 (at end of volume).

CHAPTER II
FRANÇOIS RENÉ DE CHATEAUBRIAND

I

IN turning to the author of *Memories from Beyond the Grave*, I cannot too strongly emphasise the principle which I laid down in the Introduction to these essays: that " we are not here concerned about literary and artistic quality, about the *ability* of writers." I added: " A poet who has no invention, no style, no genius, does not count. He may have an ephemeral success, but he has no lasting fame and no influence. Upon him we will not waste our time."

Certainly there is no case in which we must be more careful to avoid the least semblance of misunderstanding, by using the phrase " bad masters," than that of the opulent and noble writer, the prince of French prose, Chateaubriand. The author of *Atala*, of *René*, of the *Genius of Christianity*, and especially of the *Itinerary* and the *Historical Miscellanies*, is assuredly a great writer—if by " great writer " we mean one who has original and profound thoughts, and expresses them in a brilliant, solid, living, personal style.

Chateaubriand has equals in French prose, no doubt, but he has no superior. He is right in the first rank, in the group of sonorous and magnificent masters of words, in the company of Bossuet, Montesquieu, and Buffon. He is one of those who have given our written language that amplitude and majesty, that clearness and harmony,

43

which make it the most perfect and imperishable of modern tongues.

We may be proud of our French prose. It is the finest in the world, either the modern or the ancient world. Other nations have, perhaps, given birth to greater poets than ours. We have not, perhaps, produced one of those rare works of imagination, those almost miraculous products of a literature, which sustain the race for all time. Certain languages of the North and of the South give the poet musical rhythms, rich vocabularies, verbal colouring which the French language has not. But nowhere, either in England, Germany, or Russia, in Italy, or Spain, or Provence, or even in ancient Rome or Greece, will one find an equal to that strong and compact group of prose-writers, with their rich, powerful, supple, and alert works, who have appeared in France from Villehardouin and the Sire de Joinville, uninterruptedly, to our own time. From philosophers of the most solid character to the most sprightly story-tellers, from orators whose periods hang like folds of imperial purple to controversialists whose succinct and telling phrases flash like the play of swords, there is not a single shade of the human mind, not a single flight of the soul, not a single cry of nature, that has not found its final expression in French prose. It lends itself to the sublime aspirations of the poet no less than to the sallies of popular gaiety. It is, in turns, a chant of solemn harmony and a sparkling ripple of laughter. The blend of resonant vowels and sonorous diphthongs in its syllables, and especially the infinitely subtle play of its silent letters, make it an unrivalled instrument of richly diverse and finely measured music in the hands of the man who can play thereon.

How ridiculous it is to try to restrict the merit and

the glory of the French tongue by granting it only the
clearness of shallow water which reflects the vivacity of
the Gallic spirit ! Yes, I know that we have Montaigne,
Voltaire, and Paul Louis Courier; and no one could, I
think, admire them more than I do. But we have also
in our nation the main current of the old Roman stream,
represented by craftsmen of verbal magnificences, superb
masters of harmony and construction; and these are, in the
long run, the finest representatives of our genius. There
is nothing, even in ancient Rome, to equal the august pomp
of a Bossuet, the evenly flowing abundance of a Montesquieu, the glittering pageantry of a Buffon. Livy is
less impressive than the first; Sallust less solid than the
second; Cicero less rich than the third. Chateaubriand
completes this incomparable group.

This Breton, reared on the marrow of the classics,
combines in his sonorous, enfolding, large, and princely
style the oratorical and didactic qualities of Roman
education with the poetical virtues of the Celtic tradition.
What poem of severe rhythm is there in any tongue to
surpass this funeral chant over the death of Atala ?

I sat in silence at the foot of the couch on which Atala lay
dead. How often, in my sleep, I had nursed that dear head on
my knees ! How often had I not bent over her, to catch and
breathe her breath ! Now no sound came from her still breast.
I awaited in vain the awakening of her beauty.

The moon lent its pale torch to my watch over the dead. It
rose out of the midst of the night like a white Vestal coming to
weep over the bier of a companion. Soon it spread amongst the
woods the great secret of melancholy which it loves to tell to the
venerable oaks and to the ancient shores of the seas. From time
to time the monk dipped a flowering branch in some consecrated
water, then, shaking the moist branch, perfumed the night with
the balms of heaven. Now and again he chanted, to an old-time
air, some verses of an ancient poet named Job.·

. . . His grave, faintly modulated voice rolled through the
silence of the desert. The name of God and of the tomb broke
from all the echoes, all the torrents, all the forests. The cooing of

Virginia's dove, the fall of water on the mountain-side, the sound of the bell that summoned travellers, mingled with the funeral chant; and one seemed to hear in the groves of death the distant choir of the departed answering the voice of the hermit.

What Athenian or Roman historian ever gave us clearer thoughts, in more sober language, than those expressed in the *Itinerary*, when the great traveller visits the ruins of Athens and of Sparta ?

Here we must mention a memorable example of the superiority which literature gives to one people over another, even when the latter has displayed great virtues in war. It may be said that the battles of Leuctra and Mantinea erased the name of Sparta from the earth, while Athens retained her sovereignty, though taken by the Lacedæmonians and ravaged by Sylla. She saw hastening to her bosom the Romans who had conquered her, who now made it a glory to be counted her children. One took the name Atticus; another called himself the pupil of Plato and Demosthenes. The Latin muses, Lucretius, Horace, and Vergil, for ever chant the Queen of Greece. "I grant the dead the pardon of the living," said the greatest of the Cæsars when he forgave guilty Athens. Hadrian would add the title of Archont of Athens to that of Emperor; and he raised innumerable works of art in the land of Pericles. Constantine the Great was so flattered when the Athenians set up a statue of him that he poured favours upon the city. Julian shed tears as he left the Academy, and, when at length he triumphed, he ascribed his victory to the Minerva of Pheidias. The Chrysostoms, Basils, and Cyrils come, as Cicero and Atticus had done, to study eloquence at its source. Down to the Middle Ages Athens is called the school of learning and genius. When Europe rouses itself from barbarism, its first cry is for Athens. "What has become of it ?" is asked on every side. And when men learn that its ruins still exist, they fly to them as one does to the recovered ashes of a dead mother.

But I should be tempted to reproduce the whole of his works, so irresistible is the fascination of his style, so unforgettable is every line that he has written.

The two specimens I have quoted are enough to show that we must be deeply grateful to Chateaubriand for having unsealed once more, at the beginning of the nineteenth century, those great sources of French prose which one might have thought closed for ever; so parched and arid did our poor tongue seem in the clumsy imitators whom the glory of Voltaire had left in our fashionable literature. It is to the influence of Chateaubriand that we owe the renaissance of the true " classic " language after all the paltriness of " classicism " and decadence.

On the other hand, we know—there is no need to prove it by examples and quotations—how he raised public taste toward the beauty of epic themes and the grandeur of great thoughts. He wrote nothing that does not reveal a lofty soul and a vast brain. He was, unquestionably, a great poet.

How is it then that, after so sincere an expression of the admiration we feel for the writer, we yet venture to put Chateaubriand amongst those whose work was, in the end, depressing and devitalising? Why is he amongst those who helped to give our people troubled minds and disordered hearts?

It may seem strange that we thus inscribe the name of Chateaubriand on the list of " bad masters " while, in the same breath, we declare him in the front rank of writers and a thinker of noble cast. It is true, however. In spite of his genius—in spite of the largeness of his spirit, the loftiness of his thought, even the real services that his works have rendered to the re-emerging literature of France—Chateaubriand had a morally evil influence on subsequent generations, and still has on us; an influence all the more evil because he had no suspicion of it, because his readers and admirers have no suspicion of it, and because his fine genius, drawing all souls to itself, made him the more dangerous by his very power. Let us try, with the respect that we owe to a great writer, to ascertain the causes of this evil influence and make clear in what it consists.

II

Those who read carefully, and with genuine admiration, *René*, the *Genius of Christianity*, *Atala*, the *Itinerary*, the *Historical Miscellanies*, and especially the *Memories from Beyond the Grave*, must see that, whatever the beauty of the style, the interest of the subject, the loftiness of sentiment, the incomparable skill of the work, one is never fully satisfied as one turns over their sumptuous pages. Some strange feeling of uneasiness weighs upon the spirit of the reader. Dare we say that this strange and indefinable impression is boredom ? That would be a gross word to breathe in speaking of so great a man. Nor would it be either just or accurate, for when a man is bored he turns his back for ever upon the orator or the writer. We do not turn away from Chateaubriand. We return to him, in spite of this feeling of dissatisfaction. We are drawn back by the sumptuous richness of his style. We read and reread him incessantly. We flatter ourselves, as we read him, that we have the full joy of enthusiasm. We deliberately let ourselves be carried away by the sweep of his imagination, and the rush of his great thoughts. Yet, in spite of the profusion of qualities in his work, we remain cold, unmoved, asking ourselves why the soul is not enchanted by such a wealth of seduction.

And gradually, if we carefully consider what we feel, we discover that this uneasiness, so vague and so insuperable, comes from the fact that between the book and the reader there is a being whose constant presence prevents us from tasting the pure joy of the ideas and the beauty of the superb descriptions: a being who checks enthusiasm and forbids surrender to the charm—and this being is Chateaubriand himself.

48

François René de Chateaubriand

There is, in fact, in the whole world of letters no writer who resisted less than Chateaubriand what one may call the tyranny of one's own individuality. Even Rousseau, whose work is infested with personal sentiment, has at times impulses that carry him beyond himself. He has bursts of anger that take him away from his petty daily crises. He rises to the height of such strong and such human passions that for a moment he ceases to be Rousseau and becomes wholly a man, *man*. Chateaubriand, never. Everywhere, always, wherever he travels, whatever he sees, whether it be the banks of the Jordan or the Falls of Niagara, the Acropolis or the streets of London—whether he broods over the morals of his age or the great events of history—in face of the most tragic or the most sublime spectacles that the earth or the race affords, he remains unalterably Chateaubriand: M. le vicomte de Chateaubriand.

Even in his *Historical Studies*, the most objective and least known of his works, the one, perhaps, that contains most beauty, he cannot help but drop from time to time some of those haughty reflections, of a superb disenchantment, in which one recognises the author of the *Memories from Beyond the Grave*.

Does he devote a few lines to Trajan? Brief as the sketch is, he does not fail to insert this reflection:

This admirable prince had only the weakness of great hearts. He had too deep a love of glory !

And everybody knows the famous phrase which he penned, at Rome, in face of the ruins of a dead world:

I have again seen the Appian Way. It is like my life: an avenue of cypresses bordered with tombs.

This inability to forget one's own personality in the presence of life is a sentiment that is, in itself, often

D

barren and always pernicious. It was the great evil
of the century; scarcely a single writer escaped it. In
Chateaubriand this individualism became a most acute
malady. Through all his work it passes like the breath
of disease: a disease, indeed, full of profound charm,
the influence of which has fallen upon a whole era—
melancholy.

III

In our time the word " melancholy " has been greatly
abused. As it was very much in the fashion, and it
gave rise to vague and, seemingly, " poetical " ideas, it
was put everywhere. It was applied to men and things,
to gods and animals. It was thrust back into the past
and forward into the future. In the end men came to
confuse under the term "melancholy" all that related
to sadness, to pain, even to death.

This has gone so far that now the word has no meaning.
It is one of those general words, worn and effaced like old
coins, which contemporary writers, in their ignorance and
inaccuracy, use everywhere to fill a gap in a verse, to
frame an idle rhyme, to make a facile epithet.

Yet it once had, and ought still to have, a very precise
meaning; and it is as well to recall this if we would understand properly the particular genius and the evil influence
of Chateaubriand. The word "melancholy," in fact, though
not used so lavishly before the twentieth century, is a
very old word in our language. Our best classical writers
kept it in its place, giving it its full and limited significance.

The finest, perhaps the most conclusive, example is
found in Racine's *Bérénice*, where the lamentable
Antiochus, true precursor of the heroes of modern love,
groans at the feet of the Jewish queen:

Long lingered my footsteps in Cæsarea,
The scene where my heart by thy charm first was stirred.
Thy desolate realm answered not to my call,
And tears told my grief as I retrod thy path.
At length, a weak prey to my *melancholy*,
Despair turned my barque here to Italy's shore.

Here, in a sense, we place our finger upon the morbid and degrading idea of the word *melancholy* in precise and concrete form.

Just reflect on this case of the thwarted lover, put on the stage by Racine. One of the most deplorable characters in the whole of classic tragedy is this Antiochus weeping beside Bérénice. He is melancholy in its essence. He is the man who, incapable of struggling against sorrow, wraps himself in it as in some strong perfume. Has the woman he loves left the East? Forthwith this East, with all its teeming life and glorious light, becomes an empty and wearisome desert:

How weary my soul in this desolate East!

And he leaves this "desert of the East" to go to Rome in search of the woman who has made him suffer, who will continue to make him suffer, and by whose side he will taste the savour of suffering. That is why in the famous tirade we quoted the word used by Racine has really the entire fulness of its material and moral significance. We may say that *Bérénice* is the living picture of the evil we call *melancholy*.

What, then, *is* melancholy? How are we to define it?

Properly speaking, it is a state of mental depression which makes the man who suffers from it the victim of a fixed idea, prevents him from sharing in the active movement of the life about him, and forces him to turn over and over within him the evil with which he is infested; he not only does nothing to heal himself, but in the end he takes complacence in his malady, seeks and finds a morbid charm in it, and persuades himself that his happiness or his glory consists in attaching himself to his sorrow and clothing himself therein as in a superior elegance.

It is a malady of the soul, a vice of the spirit, a weakness of the heart. It is a lack of character and energy. When one strips it of all the poetic clouds in which it enwraps itself, melancholy is nothing but a form, the most persistent form, of moral cowardice. In other words, it is the triumph of some passion or other over the will.

Hence all the passions engender the state of melancholy when they predominate in us and take possession of our being. The fatal weakness may come of a thwarted ambition, an injured pride, an incurable envy, an insatiable hatred, an ever-grasping avarice, or a sterilising idleness; just as it may be born of a physical evil the chronic acuteness of which unceasingly besets the mind of the man who suffers from it. But of all physical and moral maladies, of all human passions, that which most of all engenders, sustains, and augments melancholy is love.

The passion of love, whether it be sensual or sentimental, violent or platonic, satisfied or thwarted, has this element of the perpetual and the irresistible, that it leaves in the heart of those whom it possesses no room for any other sentiment, no moment of forgetfulness, no escape from it to some tranquil labour. The lover can never cease to think of the object of his or her love. The man or woman who loves with the full ardour of passion is compelled either to vanquish the passion or to suffer inexorably from it. Does he conquer? Then he is strong, robust; he will rise once more to the height of

52

joy. Is he conquered ? Then he is weak, predestined
to sorrow; for he cannot but be unhappy. The one who
loves has his soul so filled with the obsession of the loved
being that at all times and in all places he is moved by
it to the degree of pain. Far from his love he suffers
that he sees her not; beside her he suffers because he
fears to lose her. If he possesses her, he suffers because
he cannot further possess her; and his very pleasures
are but crises between two sorrows. That is so because
it is the property of every passion to make a man lose
the balance of his mental powers and to destroy in him
this supreme virtue, the loftiest and fairest of all virtues,
the most fruitful in beneficent action, the true reflection
of God in man—serenity.

It follows that the passion of love, from the mere fact
that it lasts longer and that one takes delight in it, is
the one which breeds in us the most invincible melancholy. This is so true that, in the dialect of individualist
and amorous poetry, men have come to confuse the
effect with the chief of its causes, and the word "melancholy" has been used to denote that state of idle dream,
of vague tenderness, of unsated desire, which is excited
in us, first by love itself, then by the hopes, the regrets,
the weaknesses, the formless aspirations to which love
gives birth in the soul before or after its violent reign.

Thus has been created that entirely modern sentiment,
rather vague in form, but essentially morbid in its nature,
which is now called melancholy; though it, apparently,
differs a little from real melancholy. People think that
this sentiment was born but yesterday because they have
sought to give it a poetic adornment, instead of seeing in
it the source of our moral weakness.

Chateaubriand himself shall give us, in his masterly
style, the definition of this contemporary evil, with which

none was more deeply tainted than he. Here is what he says of it in his *Genius of Christianity*, in the chapter entitled " On the Vagueness of the Passions " :

We have still to speak of a state of the soul which, it seems to us, has not yet been closely studied. It is that which precedes the development of the passions, when our powers, still young, active, and entire, but confined, act only upon themselves, without aim or object. The more nations advance in civilisation, the greater becomes this condition of *vagueness* of the passions. For a very lamentable thing then happens : the large number of examples all round us, the multitude of books dealing with man and the sentiments, make men clever without experience. We are disillusioned before we have enjoyed. The desires remain, but we have no illusions. The imagination is rich, abundant, and marvellous ; life is poor, arid, and disenchanted. We live with full heart in an empty world. Without having used anything, we have abused everything.

The bitterness which this state of the soul pours over life is incredible. The heart twists and turns in a hundred ways, to use the strength which it feels to be useless. In olden times men hardly knew this secret unrest, this soreness of stifled passions which ferment together. A great political existence, the games of the gymnasium or of the Field of Mars, the business of the Forum or the mart, filled their hours, and left no room for weariness of the heart.

They were, moreover, not inclined to those exaggerations, those hopes, those aimless fears, that restlessness of ideas and sentiments, that perpetual inconstancy which is but a constant disgust ; *feelings which we acquire in the company of women.* Women, apart from the direct passion which they inspire in modern nations, have also an influence on the other sentiments. They have in their life a certain listlessness which they communicate to us. They make our manly character less resolute ; and our passions, softened by the admixture of theirs, assume at once an aspect of uncertainty and of tenderness.

In fine, since the Greeks and Romans never looked beyond this life, and never imagined pleasures more perfect than those of this world, they were not, as we are, disposed to meditation and desire by the character of their religion. Fashioned to meet our miseries and our needs, the Christian religion ever offers us the twofold picture of the sorrows of earth and the joys of heaven ; and by this means it creates in the heart a source of present evils and remote hopes, from which flow insatiable reveries. The Christian always regards himself as a traveller who here below

54

is passing through a vale of tears, and will find rest only beyond the tomb. This world is not the object of his desires, for he knows that the days of man are few and that this object would soon fail him.

The persecutions which the early faithful endured augmented in them this disgust for the things of life. The barbaric invasion completed this, and gave the mind of man an impress of sadness, perhaps even a tinge of misanthropy, that has never been effaced. On all sides arose convents to receive unhappy men and women whom the world had deceived, and souls that would rather ignore certain sentiments of life than run the risk of seeing them cruelly betrayed.

In our time, when these ardent souls have had no monasteries, or have lacked the virtue that guides one to them, they have found themselves strangers in the midst of men! Disgusted with their age, terrified by their religion, they remained in the world without abandoning themselves to the world. They then became the prey of a thousand chimeras. Then arose *that culpable melancholy* which is engendered in the midst of passions, when these passions, without aim, devour themselves in some solitary heart.

IV

Long as the quotation is, we must give it in full, for it contains the whole explanation of the impotence which made captives of most of the men of the nineteenth century. It admirably depicts that state of " vagueness of soul " which was the source of all the languorous works of the last century. It even shows the evil influence of it. But it is also curious and typical, because it enables us to see how far Chateaubriand and his contemporaries deceived themselves as to the very nature of their disease, its causes, its real ugliness; and how they lay so far under an illusion that they found distinguished, even noble, motives for their unheroic malady.

" Then arose that culpable melancholy," says Chateaubriand. By that he seems to convey that the evil was quite recent. He even says in set terms that " in olden times men hardly knew this secret unrest." We shall see presently, by examples, that they knew it very well; that the malady is as old as human weakness, of which it is an outcome. But all that remains for us, in the light of history and letters, from those earlier days is the memory of their strong and splendid ages; and in such ages melancholy, an evil with so little virility, has always been despised as a weakness and combated as a moral defect.

One of the reasons given by Chateaubriand in explanation of our modern melancholy, as opposed to the serenity of old times, is frankly childish. " A great political existence, the games of the gymnasium or of the Field of Mars, the business of the Forum or the mart, filled their hours, and left no room for weariness of the heart." This would mean that, according to the author of *René*, the men of old were not, like us, melancholic because they had a more active public life than ours. From which it seems to follow, by contrast, that if men had had occasion to live with greater intensity in the days when Chateaubriand was writing they would not have been melancholy.

Now, Chateaubriand's book was published in 1802, and it had, doubtless, been thought out and composed during the Revolution and the years of the Consulate. It will be admitted that in these circumstances the argument given by the great writer looks rather like a joke. To speak of " the great political life of the ancients," to quote " the business of the Forum or the mart," at the moment when France and Europe quivered in such a storm of violent action and political passion as humanity had never seen before—to seem to contrast the agitations of Rome and Greece with the tranquillity of the modern world under Napoleon Bonaparte, in order to justify René's melancholy—is a somewhat unexpected per-

formance. Did I not fear to depart too widely from the
noble style in which Chateaubriand addresses us, I should
be tempted to say, disrespectfully, " That's not bad."

We must find another reason for this " culpable melancholy," and, as a matter of fact, Chateaubriand seeks
another. He finds one that we should have been still
less disposed to expect—Christianity !

This time it is not merely a mistake: it is an absurdity.
The claim is all the stranger because it is made in the
heart of a book that is devoted to the defence of Christianity. It is a singular way of defending a moral
institution to make it the source of the greatest moral
perturbations ! If it were true, as Chateaubriand says,
that Christianity had inevitably engendered melancholy
in the souls of men, we should be compelled to reject
it at once as a mischievous doctrine: to condemn it for
ever, not merely in the present, but in the past and the
future. Every morality that enfeebles the soul is immoral. Every religion that enervates the heart is
unworthy of a divine ideal.

Now, whether one is a Christian or no, even if one is
an atheist or deist, there is one thing proved by the
whole of history—namely, that in the development of the
ages, which it sustained, Christianity was a source of
strength, of energy, of fruitful activity, of virility, even
of heroism. By the lever of faith which it put in the
souls of men it displaced nations and continents. One
may or may not esteem the human work which it inspired,
but at least it had a prodigious vitality, and instead of
plunging the soul in " insatiable reveries," as the author
of *Atala* says, Christianity evoked a formidable movement. The clearest manifestations of Christianity were
the saints, the apostles, the heroes: Paul, Jerome, Augus-
tine, Dominic, Francis of Assisi, Bruno, Bernard, Peter

the Hermit, Vincent de Paul, Loyola—the greatest stirrers of men who ever were. They were Gregory VII., Dante, Luther, Sixtus V., Bossuet, Pius IX.—masters of intellectual strength and moral energy. They were Roland, Godfrey, Tancred, Cervantes, Bayard, Christopher Columbus—all the paladins and knights of the great Crusades. That is what Christianity produced: men who, instead of groaning over earthly life and passing through it as through " a vale of tears," joyfully and courageously embraced its duties and trials, and developed all the strength that was entrusted to them.

Chateaubriand is profoundly mistaken in trying to make Christianity responsible for modern melancholy. Such a Christianity would be a degenerate religion for women, for invalids, for the impotent. It is elsewhere, at some lower level, that we must look for the real cause of melancholy. Chateaubriand could not find it; because, irremediably tainted with the evil himself, he sought rather to invest it with some prestige than see in it a real weakness. This cause, the only cause, is simply the vice, eternal in humanity, but especially virulent in morbid societies, of individualism.

V

It would be a curious error to regard the era of melancholy as opening in the present age, or even in modern times. In every age, in every civilisation, there were diseased beings who wilfully avoided the active and strong life, and isolated and charmed themselves in the intoxicating and solitary contemplation of their personal sorrows.

Without lingering over historical personalities, whose imperfectly known conduct might be a subject of controversy, let us simply take the heroes of the most ancient literatures: those, especially, who have been immortalised by the greatest of poems, in which are reflected the ways of the human race. It will readily be granted that such works as the Bible, the *Iliad*, the *Odyssey*, and the poems of Sophocles, Euripides, and Aristophanes, are the most precious testimonies we could have in regard to the moral ideas of the ancient world. We may be badly informed, from scantiness of documents, about the life and character of the kings and men who really lived in former times. But when we turn to the heroes created by the poets, we know infallibly what spirit it was that animated them, for their life, outer and inner, has come down to us in its entirety.

The greatest and most splendid example of a hero tainted with melancholy is presented to us in the *Iliad*, in the person of the impetuous Achilles. What is the famous sulking of Achilles in his tent after the departure of Briseis and the affront from Agamemnon but the sentiment of melancholy at its clearest ? Is it not, as we defined it, " that state of mental depression which makes the man who suffers from it the victim of a fixed idea, prevents him from sharing in the active movement of the life about him, and forces him to turn over and over the evil with which he is infested, so that he not only does nothing to heal himself, but in the end takes complacence in his malady "? Is not that precisely the case of the angry and sulking Achilles ?

They have taken away his captive and hurt his self-esteem. And so night and day he sits aloof from the stir and the combat, lingers groaning in the camp, remains deaf to all the roar of the battles. What to him is the death of his comrades, the imminent rout of the Greeks ? He has a personal sorrow; the world is nothing to him In vain do the ambassadors of Greece, Ulysses, Ajax, even his tutor, the sage Phenix, come to entreat him to forget his own grief and think only of the public calamity. Achilles will not hear. He replies:

Prince of peoples, illustrious Ajax, son of Telamon, all thy speech seems to me to be dictated by reason; *but my breast swells with anger when I recall him who affronted me amongst the Greeks.*

And the ambassadors, failing in their mission, return in sadness to the camp of the Greeks, while Achilles angrily hugs his savage melancholy.

For what reason does the impetuous and passionate young prince refuse to join the common life and stubbornly stand aside ? A purely personal reason: an excess of sensitiveness and pride, an exaggerated sentiment of his own personality. He sets his own grief against that of all the Hellenes. He puts his little injuries in the scale with the destiny of his race. Perish Greece, as long as the passions of Achilles are satisfied. He is a striking example of individualism in his sulking.

Let us pass to another hero, of the same literature and the same cycle, Philoctetes. He also is a glaring example of the evil that may be evoked in a soul, even an heroic soul, by this insidious melancholy. Without lingering over all the different interpretations of the character of Philoctetes which the poets have given us, let us take the most distinguished—that of Sophocles.

Philoctetes is on the Isle of Lemnos, a prey to two sorrows: the wound to his foot, which makes him lame, on the one hand, and, on the other, the terrible hatred he has sworn to the Atrides and the great Ulysses. An irritable and selfish genius, like Achilles, he deems that his self-esteem has been affronted, and it is from this moral wound that he suffers most. He turns it over and over, complacently, in his solitude at Lemnos, and will do nothing to heal it. In vain does Neoptolemus, the

messenger of the Greeks, come to entreat him to set out
for Troy, where Philoctetes will be able at one and the
same time to save the Achæan army and assuage his
own grief. He refuses, because his hatred of Ulysses
and Agamemnon is stronger than the desire of relief.
Whatever the terms of peace they offer him, he replies:
" Sooner would I listen to the odious viper that lamed me."

The resentment in his heart seems to him more pleasant
than the health of his body or the glory of his name.
He cries:

> Sacred land, and ye gods who see all, chastise them some day;
> *chastise them all, if ye have any pity for me !* Ye see my wretched
> life. Let them perish from before my eyes, and I shall be healed
> of my evils !

Is this not the perfect character of melancholy, with
its morbid charm, its fixed idea, and, above all, the same
hypertrophy of self which we found in Achilles ? " Perish
all they who despise the wound on my foot," cries
Philoctetes; a proof that he considers his personal injury
a graver thing than the destiny of the Greeks. One
might even find something of the melancholy which we
call modern in the hero of Sophocles, whose heart is so
far from noble—namely, the diseased sentiment of nature
which melancholy in the end always engenders in those
who abandon themselves to its unwholesome inebriation.
Philoctetes murmurs:

> Farewell, dear cave that has sheltered me ! Farewell, ye
> sparkling streams that water these vast plains ! Farewell, wild
> tumult of the sea breaking upon the promontories, whose foam,
> borne on the wind, came so often to moisten my head ! And thou,
> Mount Hermeon, who didst send back to me so oft the echo of
> my groans. . . .

Do we not seem to hear, long before his time, some
romantic person of the Byron school calling upon nature
to witness his woes ? It is a proof that the same causes

always beget the same effects; that the lyricism of strong individualism issues, in every age, in the same frantic exaggerations.

Here, then, are two striking models of melancholy in Greece itself, even heroic Greece. And in both cases we see that the cause is the same: the excessive cult of personality, which is put above social life.

It would be easy to discover the same truth when we pass from Greek literature to the Bible. If there is one famous exhibition of melancholy in the Scriptures, it is the series of reflections, thoughts, and meditations which bear the name *Ecclesiastes*. Here we have, perhaps, the most complete and most incurable melancholy that ever was. Our modern romantics are petty fools beside the royal pessimist who wrote:

The day of death is better than the day of one's birth. . . . Sorrow is better than laughter, for by the sadness of the countenance the heart is made better.

This is beyond Chateaubriand, Byron, Macpherson, or even Baudelaire. And what is the habitual frame of mind of the man who wrote these thoughts of Ecclesiastes? A perpetual concern with, an unceasing anxiety about, his own personality apart from society. He speaks of the race only in so far as it can do good or evil to the individual. One feels that in the eyes of Ecclesiastes this frail being, hardly able to survive for five or six decades, counts for infinitely more than all empires, all races, and all civilisations. Only the troubles and weaknesses of the individual interest him:

What profit hath a man of all his labour which he taketh under the sun?

In point of fact, what does he get? Sickness, decay, old age, and death. Says Ecclesiastes:

One generation passeth away, and another generation cometh: but the earth abideth for ever.

And the plaintive prophet can find no consolation. What! *He* must go into nothing, and the flowers shall continue to bloom ? And the stars shall still shine ? And new generations shall come to smile upon ever new-born life ? A terrible thing, is it not, not to be able to take the whole universe with one when one has to go. Of a truth, all is indeed vanity.

This philosophy of disenchantment, which men have admired with open mouths for ages, is, at the bottom, no more than a rather childish grievance because one is not the centre of the world. When I was a child, I used to shake the trees, and I was surprised, nay indignant, that I did not cause a wind. . . .

Let these suffice as examples. They are typical. Whatever form melancholy assumes, savage or tender, violent or indolent, proud or amorous, its single source is the exaggeration of one's own personality. It comes of individualism.

If an individual regards himself as the centre of the world, he is bound to be sad, for everything about him shows him that he is nothing. However desperately he clings to fugitive things, fills his eyes with ephemeral splendours, and intoxicates himself with fleeting pleasures, everything passes away and flies away. As our dear Ecclesiastes says: " All the rivers run into the sea: yet the sea is not full." That is why individualism leads to sadness, and why the sadness is unclean when it is a permanent frame of mind, when it becomes a definitive melancholy.

Strong men, true heroes, are not sad. Great sorrows fall upon them as they fall upon other men; and perhaps their responsive hearts feel more deeply than do the hearts of the weak. But they rise again, after the blow, hide the sorrow within themselves, keep it from the eyes of others instead of solemnly draping themselves in it and posing as melancholics. They do more than resign themselves to the evil; they accept it. And, shaking their souls, they go back into life, knowing well that all pain is inevitable, and that it ought not to disturb the work of man longer than the storm disturbs the majestic march of the days and the seasons. They know that they are part of the universal life, and that, consequently, their personal griefs must, in the general evolution of the world, be but accidents for themselves alone.

Take two of the most complete heroes who have ever been immortalised in poetic masterpieces, the Ulysses of Homer and the Æneas of Vergil. Surely here we have the very types of the strong and deliberate man, inaccessible to melancholy, yet very accessible to human emotion ! Whatever misfortunes assail them, they stand erect and march ever onward. Kingdoms destroyed, vessels lost, dear comrades carried off by death, loving women whose smile they miss but whose rule they know they must fear—they leave everything aside in their heroic advance; not without deep suffering, but they are strengthened by the robustness of their virile mission. Circe may spread the splendid magic of her palaces; the sirens may sing; Dido may weep in vain on the shore. They go down toward the task that awaits them: one toward that model of the Greek city, the Ithaca of tradition, where father, spouse, and son await him, the other toward the future greatness of the Roman people. And their life of movement and adventure, a hard life, full of difficulties, gives such consolation, thanks to their courage, that, in spite of all their trials and sorrows, the final impression they leave on us is one of joy.

These great poems are, in fact, works of supreme joy, in which heroic souls move. One feels that all the fulness of life is in them, because in them life, with all its passing sorrows, with the certain prospect of death, is accepted with an unwavering heart. It is strength and joy that radiate from the *Odyssey* and the *Æneid*. It is a radiant joy that illumines Dante's *Paradise*, after the terrible trial of his *Hell*. It is joy that the increasing beauty of *Don Quixote* communicates to us by its generous spirit. And the entire race that passes through the pages of Rabelais fills his profound work with a bracing joyousness.

One may, indeed, after an impartial examination, draw up these two formulæ, for books and for men:

The deeper the poet's sense of social life, the stronger he becomes, the more firmly he represses sadness.

The more the poet isolates himself in his vain personality, the feebler he becomes, the more he yields to melancholy.

VI

This evil of melancholy, eternal as human weakness, is particularly rife in periods of disturbance and transition. We shall inquire later how it is that France and Europe were invaded by a universal sadness at the close of the eighteenth century. Everybody was tainted by it. Some resisted, and gradually rid themselves of the taint. Others remained sick with it. Of these Chateaubriand is the most remarkable.

That is why, with all his eloquence, all his loftiness of standard, all his grandeur of style and his indisputable genius, he was the real master of modern melancholy, and therefore a " bad master."

This sickly exaltation of personality, which the wild ways of Rousseau made so tumultuous, and at times so inoffensive because of its very excess, has been invested by Chateaubriand with all the charm of his style, all the majesty of his attitude, even with some semblance of grandeur. Not once, either in his life or in his work, did Chateaubriand cease to be the haughty and disenchanted creator of René, the melancholic traveller through the avenues of history and over the plains of life.

There were other works, it is true, that were more mischievous than *René* or *Atala :* notably Goethe's *Werther.* But Goethe emerged from sadness, and became, above all, the Olympian and classic poet, the apostle, rather the high priest, of serenity. The man who penned this formula, " By classic I mean what is healthy and by romantic what is unhealthy," could not remain melancholic.

It was this journey to Rome, in his thirty-sixth year, that proved for Goethe a revelation and a restoration, and inaugurated that splendid evolution which was to transform the author of *Werther* into the author of *Faust.* He said at Rome:

I perceive, after many years, that I am like an architect who would build a tower on bad foundations, and I now wish to know well the base on which I build.

And as tranquillity, with increasing manhood, sinks deeper into his soul, he cries:

At Rome I found myself for the first time in harmony with myself: *I felt happy and reasonable.*

Such a formula effaces for ever the juvenile folly of *Werther.*

Lamartine also begins, like Goethe, with works which reflect the environing melancholy. He, too, speaks of despair and death, and cries:

What evil have I done that I deserved to be born !

At all events, turning to " the course of the fleeting hours,"
he showers invectives upon time, as it passes and carries
away our joys and sorrows:

> Jealous time! Can it be that these moments of joy
> In which love fills our cup with a full happiness
> Fly from us to the void on the same fleeting wing
>   As the days of distress ?

We find this individualism of lyrical poetry, in almost the
same words, in Victor Hugo, in his youth:

> Answer me, thou green vale: answer me, solitude,
> Nature fair to this desert of loveliness wed;
> When we sleep side by side in the calm attitude
> Which the tomb grants at last to the dumb pensive dead;
> Shall we still have the power in the grave where we lie
> To know that our bodies are dead like our loves,
> Yet go on with the feast 'neath some tranquil new sky,
> Go on with the song and the smile in fresh groves ?

That is, assuredly, the exaltation of individualism in
revolt against the laws of nature.

But Lamartine and Hugo were, like Goethe, healed,
as they grew older, of this feminine weakness; the works
of their manhood glow with virility. One writes the
Harmonies, that magnificent flight of man beyond himself to God. The other displays the serene majesty of
unbroken humanity in the *Legend of the Ages*. Neither
Lamartine nor Hugo was a source of disturbance and
weakness, whatever literary defects the severer critics
may find in them. On the contrary, the example they
give by their work and life, as they develop, inspires
strength and drives away sadness.

Chateaubriand, however, never removed from his
shoulders the dark cloak of night which invests the
romanticism of *René*. All life long he took with him
the disenchantment of personal pride. He bore it from
the cascades of America to the monuments of Rome,

from the streets of London to the deserts of Palestine, from the ruins of Greece to the Government offices of Paris. Even in his last, and posthumous, work, the *Memories from Beyond the Grave*, he cannot divest himself of his sickly and devouring vanity. It is always himself that he puts on the chief pedestal amidst the crowd of events and men, upon whom he pours his saddened disdain. As Sainte-Beuve says, " in all his works he is René."

We may apply to the whole of Chateaubriand's work these words which he puts into the mouth of Father Souël in *René :*

> It is only from inability to see far enough that one hates men and life. Look a little farther, and you will soon be convinced that all these evils which you lament are mere nothings. . . . Whoever has received strength must devote it to the service of his fellows. If he leaves it unused, he is first punished with a hidden misery, and sooner or later Heaven sends him some frightful chastisement.

I do not know whether Heaven took the trouble to send some " frightful chastisement " upon M. le vicomte de Chateaubriand. The beauty of his style and the nobleness of his life ought to have procured indulgence for him. It does seem, however, that he was " punished with a hidden misery." The misfortune is that by the magic of his words he has communicated this misery to three or four generations of admirers.

HONORÉ DE BALZAC

Balzac seems to have been not so much an observer of the
society of his own day as one who helped to form a new society.
—Paul Bourget.

CHAPTER III

HONORÉ DE BALZAC

I

THE hour is badly chosen, I confess, for dealing with the author of the *Human Comedy*. His fame was never so widespread, never so unchallengeable. By a process of mutual suggestion, such as crowds are susceptible to at certain periods of history, everybody incites each, and each incites everybody, to make the great novelist a sort of idol which must not be touched, the cult of which is at once a patriotic exaltation and an international communion. In face of him all judgment is suspended, all expression is forbidden; except that one may shake one's head and close one's eyes and murmur, with an air of intelligence: " Balzac !"

He has on his side the respect of the Institutes and the enthusiasm of the cafés. The boulevard admires him no less than the banquet. Revolutionaries and Conservatives vie with each other for him, or, rather, share him. Business men, who despise letters, deign to admit that he is " very good." To complete his success, they are raising somewhere the pedestal on which his glory will shine; and the distinguished corporation of men of letters prepares, in solemn pomp, to canonise its patron. The man who stands aloof looks as if he wanted to make himself eccentric by uttering a solitary protest. Now, I have no taste for such an attitude. The use of paradoxes, from a mere desire to astonish the gallery, seems to me a game for rhetoricians, a piece of worldly vanity. It does not in the least displease me that I think as others do; and when it chances that the opinion I hold is that of the whole world, I am not irritated, but as pleased as when I see a light reflected in a hundred mirrors.

If then, by the very terms of these studies, I am now compelled to put Balzac in the category of bad masters, it is in no sense a protest against the forthcoming statue. I have long held the view which I am now about to propound: that, namely, Balzac has had a deplorable influence upon our mentality, and that, in spite of all his genius, indeed by force of his genius, he has wrought great evil.

For the rest, I hasten to add that, with this moral reserve, I think the admiration of men of letters and of the crowd for that wonderful writer natural and legitimate. What a colossus! It has often been said, and I repeat it because in fact he *was* a colossus, and that there is no other way of saying it. Industry, observation, imagination, vision, work, influence—everything about him was colossal. His mind absorbed the world, and he created it anew from top to bottom. What power of invention and movement! His genius was a miracle of the human race. What ancestral store of observation and secular tradition had he that enabled him to pull, at will, all the guiding strings of the social comedy, and in the course of a few years learn, possess, and lay bare the tangle of motives in our most secret actions? We know not. We are overwhelmed in presence of this gigantic work, fascinated by this giddy vortex of beings and things, dominated by this creative force, vanquished and charmed, until we forget ourselves, by the glamour of the living kaleidoscope which plays unceasingly before our helpless imagination.

Genius is an occult power; but we may say of the genius

of Balzac that there is something magical about it. To listen to him is to belong to him. Happy, or unhappy— as you will—the man who enters the enchanted palaces of his work. He is overcome and carried away. He becomes a captive, without resistance and without will, passing, breathless, from labyrinth to labyrinth, so subtly fitted with his bonds that, far from perceiving them, he is intoxicated by his slavery and dreads deliverance.

Only this week as, full of my subject, I read once more a few pages of his most famous novels, to fix the essential ideas of them, I could not stop at the limited amount of reading which I had proposed, though I have long been familiar with his works. I went on from seduction to seduction, weakly forgetful of my task, and read for hours with increasing delight, so triumphant was the charm.

Yet an hour comes when the charm is broken, and then, as soon as the first confusion of one's memory has cleared, one has the right to pull oneself together, banish the pictures from one's mind, and ask what one has gained from the adventure.

Well, any man who has the courage to search thus in his soul, after carefully reading Balzac, will discover in the depths of his being a vague uneasiness, as if he had just left some busy and noisy city, after traversing one by one its hot, sombre streets, its casinos and festive drawing-rooms flooded with light and noise, and solitary rooms where despised genius and virtue keep themselves far from the crowd. He feels that he is in a troubled atmosphere, in which mingle the mustiness of vice, the acrid odour of crime, the hot breath of violent ambition and victorious passion, and—here and there—the light perfume of hidden lilies. He is very far from the sunny and bracing atmosphere that spreads from the works of a Homer, a Vergil, a Dante, a Shakespeare, or a Rabelais.   When a man reads *them*, he seems to drink some magic wine

> That lifts the human clod,

as Mistral says in his fine verse.   It seems as if a great wind, sweeping away infection, comes to us from a sea of vast expanse and rolling waves.   It seems as if our heart grows larger in our breast; that it is going to become at once large enough and light enough to take us out of ourselves and put us on the road that heroes tread.

But perhaps it would be wrong to remain too long under the first impression that Balzac makes upon us. Perhaps he has but ventured into the dark depths of life in order to light them up with his blazing torch.   After all, the poet has the absolute right to go where he pleases. There is no place into which he may not penetrate.   He may, as Dante did, brave the panthers and tigers that guard the gates of hell.   He may, as Shakespeare did, sit on the witch's stool.   All that we ask is that, wherever he goes, he shall be himself, superior to the passions that surround him: luminous in the shade, calm in the tumult, moved but never disturbed, merciful but never an accomplice, his head always radiant and divine, even when his feet sink in all the slime of humanity.

Such the poet remains: such he must make us, whom he dominates.   He must give us his own talisman in order that we may pass with him through the circles into which he takes us.   Like Dante by the side of Vergil, we must walk unscathed with him through all the turmoil of the damned.   Such does he issue from his human exploration, his brow to the skies; such must we issue with him, showing no trace of the flames we traversed, throwing off the last wisps of the smoke of the abyss, turning our eyes to the stars.

Is that the state of soul in which we come from the
works of Balzac ? We have only to ask it to find the
disturbing influence of the *Human Comedy* increasing
within us.

II

Yes, I know quite well what the answer will be: that
in Balzac there is everything—evil as well as good, cupidity
and self-denial, blackguards and heroes, frightful ambitions and delicate souls, the whole of life, in a word,
and that it is for us to make our choice in this infinitely
varied microcosm.

It would really be too easy, it would be a piece of
childish dilettantism, to cast a work of great diversity
thus into the world and say to each: " Take your choice."
It is not our place to choose: it is for the poet to impose
his choice upon us. Properly speaking, there is no choice
to make. Each part must harmonise with every other
to form a whole which will, sooner or later, make upon the
crowd a synthetic impression, good or evil, by which a
work becomes an integral part of the human mind.

Well, here is a work before us. It has had an influence
for fifty years, and it is as fresh to-day as it was in the
first year. What is the dominant note of the work, and
what does it do in our souls ? That is the only question
that matters. The rest is but idle chatter of the schools.

The dominant note of Balzac's work is the exaltation
of social life in its most tortured, its harshest and vainest
elements. Do not let us be led astray by confused
theories. Let us see things in their raw truth. Who are
Balzac's favourite heroes, the men upon whom he spends
all the magic of his imagination, whom he follows through
life with a visible tenderness ? Are they lofty idealists,
disdainful of honours and material pleasures, athirst for

justice and beauty, ready to attempt everything for the
accomplishment of something great ?   Are they liberators
of souls, inspirers of noble actions, men of self-denial,
devotion, and self-sacrifice ?   Oh no !   Men of that type
may appear in his works, but their voices are stifled by the
victorious clamours of others to whom he awards all the
splendours and all the triumphs, others who alone are
heard by the crowd in the end.   I mean that brilliant
and blustering group of which Rastignac is the most
illustrious example.

Rastignac !   There is the supreme hero of Balzac, the
man who dominates and synthetises his work as Ulysses
does that of Homer, Prometheus that of Æschylus, and
Æneas that of Vergil.   Rastignac, that accomplished
model of ferociously elegant adventurers !   Rastignac,
and the whole troop of young wolves following at his heels
for the secret plunder of life, those are the beings whom
Balzac cast alive into the circulation of souls; and he will
bear for ever the lamentable responsibility for them.

I agree that he created others.   But just examine these
others and see what little weight they have in the *Human
Comedy* beside the handsome adventurers.   It is a distressing fate for our poet, an unalterable condemnation of
his glory, that he could never draw the silhouette of a
really great man without some failure which makes it
ridiculous, while he caresses and makes perfect the figures
of his bandits.

Louis Lambert dies worn out, almost insane, on the
threshold of an impossible life.   Balthazar Claës ruins his
wife and ends in insanity.   Michel Chrestien perishes
useless and unknown.   The great poet Daniel d'Arthez
is an idiot in the world, the sport of women.   Zéphirin
Marcas languishes in obscurity and squalor. Père
Schmucke, ridiculous and ingenuous, lets himself be

robbed like a child.   Albert Savarus, powerless to realise his great hopes, flies to the Grande Chartreuse.

These are mere germs of true heroes.   See what becomes of the others, the adventurers, the devourers !

In their case there is no fear of the character-sketch being left unfinished or unskilful.   What life, what security, what movement, what adventures, for these gay folk !   For them the pleasures, the honours, the favours of women, the admiration or envy of men, the tinsel of glory, the inebriation of power, and I know not what lightness of mind and heart which makes all happiness seem but their due and invests even their misfortunes with a romantic splendour.   Look at them—Lousteau, Blondet, Bixion, the seductive Marsay, the charming De Trailles, the bold Du Tillet, the melancholic and languorous Lucien de Rubempré.   How these are decked with all the graces and all the gifts !   How they pass by in a whirl of light !   How one feels an irresistible impulse to follow them, to taste with them all the pleasures of earth, even if one must, like Lucien, die in youth from excess of love !

And the greatest of them all, the master, the conqueror, His Excellency Eugène de Rastignac, minister, count and peer of France !   What a magnificent figure !   How he haunts, like some obsessing vision, the minds of all who see him pass !

But I am wrong.   There is a still greater man in Balzac's work.   There is a more powerful being than Rastignac himself, a hero whose majestic stature rises above all the others.   And this titan of Balzac's epic, victorious like Agamemnon, subtle and wise like Ulysses, bold like Achilles, a creator like Æneas, so colossal that we stand open-mouthed before his "genius" (for he *is* a genius), is the formidable Vautrin; Vautrin the thief, Vautrin the forger, Vautrin the poisoner, Vautrin the assassin, Vautrin the convict turned policeman.

Those are the real paladins of the *Human Comedy;* all the others, all the virtuous chimeras, are but wavering shadows.

Do not tell me that Balzac is not responsible for this state of things; that it is not his fault if the world belongs to unscrupulous scoundrels rather than to noble characters and generous hearts. Do not tell me that he has been merely the passive mirror of life, the faithful painter of a social order, the gifted scribe of sovereign truth.

He a mirror? He a painter? He a mere collector of documents? What folly—or what sophistry! No writer was ever more inventive, more theoretical, more of a generaliser, more completely creative than Balzac. It was from his own brain that he derived his world, and he propped it up constantly by reasoning. He could not describe a trousers button without at once developing a theory of costume in all ages. His work teems with general ideas; often they clog the narrative. He could, as he willed, make the children of his brain higher or lower. He could arrange his creation according to any hierarchy that pleased him. He had the sovereign faculty of directing, according to his own soul, the sentiments which his heroes evoke in us.

Very well, I ask if in the whole of his work there is a single page in which one detects on the part of Balzac a shudder of revolt or disgust at his bold and ferocious adventurers? Does he endeavour to put us on our guard against the brilliant world in which he places their development? Quite the contrary. How he caresses them! How he discovers at every step they take some marvellous and indisputable theory to sustain and encourage their march to fortune! He loves them, these

78

favourite heroes of his. He loves them, not as a great-hearted poet, full of pity, may love every living thing, even when it has fallen into the most servile moral decay. No, he loves them as they are, and for what they are. He likes them to be handsome, to be bold, to please, to shine, to succeed.

Above all, to succeed; for that seems to be, in Balzac's eyes, the one aim of human life. He leaves to others the irresistible enthusiasm which in the end, in spite of his early ingenuousness, begets a Don Quixote in the heroic soul of Cervantes; the censures of Alcestis upon rogues and intriguers; the scorn of a Tartufe or the lash laid upon a Trissotin. In Balzac, Don Quixote is killed in early youth. As to Alcestis, he shall have consolation in the chatter of salons. Tartufe, a man of genius, is not arrested by the officer. He founds a bank, directs a party, guides the world from the depths of his office. Orontes is no longer ridiculous: he is king of the elegances, and sits enthroned at the feasts. Trissotin guides public opinion. There is no longer any indignation at intrigue or roguery. Such things belong to another age. Now we admire the man who wins, whatever path he has taken.

Now, is this not a piece of supreme corruption, dangerous in different fashion than is the immorality of the sensual works at which sensitive prudes take alarm? The man who corrupts the senses is, of course, guilty; but far more guilty is he who corrupts character; for if the one, by softening us, prevents us from fulfilling a generous destiny, the other incites us to mischievous enterprises by putting before us, from the time of our entry into life, the mirage of towering ambitions.

If, then, we would sum up what remains to us from all the immense work of the *Human Comedy*, the spell of which has bound us for fifty years, we find, in the last analysis, a most pernicious state of mind, most ferociously earthly and material, most removed from all nobleness, heroism, and idealism. It is a state of mind that we may resume in two words: blind admiration of good fortune, frenzied cultivation of success.

III

Did Balzac intend his work to have such a conclusion ? Did he deliberately engender, or at least support with all the aid of his genius, so mischievous and brutally positive a morality ? Certainly not. There is no question whatever but that the author of *Louis Lambert, Séraphita,* and *La Recherche de l'absolu* had a very high ideal. Quite sincerely he meant to achieve a synthetic work the crown of which should be the exaltation of the noblest impulses.

It is he who formulated this sublime æsthetic in a few lines of his *Introduction to the Study of Morals :*

It is not enough to be a man: one must be a system.

And he adds:

It is not enough to observe and think: one must observe and think with a definite object.

What object ? He tells us in these words:

In order to induce our age to accept a reflection of itself in a vast mirror, it was necessary to give it hope. The writer had to show himself a consoler when the world was cruel, to mix no shame with our dreams, to pour balm into our hearts when he had moved us to tears. In fine, he should never dismiss the spectator from the theatre without some happy thought, letting him think that man was really good when we had depicted him as bad, great when he was small. . . . It was necessary to find literary resources in the unity of virtue.

Here, surely, is a magnificent programme: perhaps a little excessive. Yet it is not enough for Balzac, who adds:

The mission of the artist is also to create great types and to raise the beautiful to the level of the ideal.

One can imagine oneself reading Corneille! Never was the " mission "—it is Balzac's own word—of the poet more clearly defined. How is it, then, that, after setting out on so fine an adventure, Balzac never realised his high destiny ? Can anyone understand why, feeling thus that he ought to be and would be one of the most radiant of torch-bearers, he stopped by the way before the sparkle of social life ? How are we to explain his lingering to celebrate the pomp of worldly glory, and to exalt as a fruitful energy the gross rut of the instincts for the most vulgar possessions ?

We must, unfortunately, tell the truth. Although he had so fine a mind and so sensitive a heart, Balzac had a mediocre soul and a hesitating character. He was the first victim of the deductions with which he adorned his own universe. He breathed the atmosphere of the world he created, and he was not sufficiently master of it to inhale it with impunity.

He shared the cupidities of his ambitious heroes, the vanity of those who loved tinsel and glory; he envied the conquests of the conquerors of life. He would himself have liked to have the gold and the power which he made the objects in life of his creatures.* What did he not do to build up a fortune rapidly ? Did he not dream of becoming a business man ?

Moreover—which is stranger—this great mind and great genius had a most foolish respect for the *parvenu*.

* See Note 3 (at end of volume).

To use a familiar English word, the author of *Lost Illusions* was a " snob." He believed in the social hierarchies and was delighted with worldly elegance. " He is a provincial," Flaubert said of him; " luxury astonishes him." He was dazed by those who succeeded in shining in the world by skill or wit, even, or especially, when these bold individuals were the fruit of his own brain.

That is why, in spite of the amount and variety of his work, it is the unhealthy part of it to which he devoted most care, and it is that part which has most influence. It is, in the long run, by its result that we must gauge a work, especially when, as in the case of Balzac, it is large and powerful enough to create a state of mind. And here it rises before us, clear and unmistakable; it is modern society. Balzac's world has left his books and come to live amongst us. His heroes are now our masters.

A writer of high authority, and one who will not be suspected of ill-feeling toward Balzac, M. Paul Bourget, very justly said:

> It has been observed that Balzac's heroes, both in literature and life, appeared especially after the death of the novelist. *Balzac seems to have been not so much an observer of the society of his own day as one who helped to form a new society.*

Nothing is more true, and nothing more terrible, as regards the responsibility of the great poet. Certainly the distinguished author of *L'Étape* would be surprised to find me quoting him as a witness against one for whom he had a filial admiration. Yet in formulating the phrase I have quoted M. Bourget has brought one of the most crushing of charges against Balzac.

Yes, it is to the author of the *Human Comedy* that we owe the ever-growing assault of the grossest ambitions, and this whole storm of insatiable cupidities which hurls the entire regiment of the emancipated, from one end of France to the other, toward power or money. It is he who goes out over the provinces of France with the magic of his works and pours into the ready ears of plebeians, already tired of their native places, an appeal to attempt to conquer Paris. It is he, in fine, who, by the glamour of his characters and the subtlety of his theories, has evoked from the troubled depths of our race that innumerable and mischievous type whose buzzing is the plague of our country and the disgrace of the modern spirit—the *parvenu*, the careerist.

There you have the real son of Balzac, the supreme product of the *Human Comedy*. Look at him. He is everywhere. He is in the salons, looking for a dowry, or in the boudoirs, looking for something worse. He orates in the Chamber, or howls in the Exchange. You find him, ready for any piece of servility, in editorial offices, and, ready for any sort of meanness, in the ante-chambers of ministers. He is on view at the theatres every first night and at every ceremony where he can get some advertisement for his vanity or advancement for his career. He is young, he is old; he is complaisant, he is insolent; he is poor, he is rich; he is a boisterous gambler, he is quietly ambitious. He is, in a word, everywhere and in every form; but you can recognise him always by this characteristic—he is invariably the courtier of success.

Naturally, this creature always existed; but at least in former times he more or less concealed himself, and gave his cupidity the air of a noble ambition. Why should he conceal himself now ? Is he not sure of the world's indulgence and admiration ? Is he not in conformity with the theories of the wise ? Is he not a hero—*Balzac's hero ?*

Unfortunately, whether he wished it or no, it has been

the fortune of the novelist to put the stamp of respectability upon all pirates on the grand scale. Ask the crowd what is its idea of one of Balzac's heroes. The reply will always be the same. All will say that it is the man who gets rid of common morality, and devotes all his energy to the task of succeeding in the world by the most adventurous means.

Has some millionaire ruined whole families in making his own fortune? A Balzac hero. Has some journalist made wealth by selling his pen? A Balzac hero. Has some juggler with money come out of jail and risen high in the banking world? A Balzac hero. Is this other openly accused by everybody of cheating and blackmail, yet has the red ribbon in his button-hole? A Balzac hero. They are all heroes of the Balzac type. The crown was put upon his glory, some years ago, when the Humbert family perpetrated their colossal fraud, with distinguished persons as their accomplices, and there was but one cry from the crowd: "Balzac heroes!" And forthwith everybody admired them.

That, in fact, is the great evil: people admire them. Anger against great filibusters is now not merely changed into indulgence; it has given place to admiring astonishment. And it is to Balzac we owe this.

I understand now why there was such a long delay in erecting the famous statue. It was necessary first for the world created by the poet to be fully developed. This is now accomplished, and the monument may dazzle the eye. On the day of the unveiling they will all be there, no doubt: Lousteau and Tillet, Trailles and Bixion, Blondet and even Rubempré—now too wise to kill himself before his fortune is made. Vautrin with his red tie, Rastignac with orders on his breast, Carentin with the tricolour round his waist, Nucingen in his new motor-car—they will all be there. They may bespatter as they please the world they have conquered, and the triumphant cry of their victory will rise in words of gratitude to their great patron. And he, the poor great man, the author of *Séraphita*, if he answers the appeal of the souls he has fashioned, and returns for a moment to put life into those bronze eyes, will see at once the extent of his fault and the cruelty of his punishment.

HENRI BEYLE (STENDHAL)

I have lived long enough to know that difference engenders hatred.—*The Red and the Black.*

CHAPTER IV
HENRI BEYLE (STENDHAL)

I

I WILL not waste my time in an attempt to compare the author of the *Human Comedy* with the author of the *Chartreuse de Parme*. It seems now to be the fashion—there are fashions even in the literary tribe—to put them both on the same level. But let us pass on. A time inevitably comes when everything resumes its real proportions, and is registered at its correct weight. Meantime, let us, like everybody else, put Stendhal by the side of Balzac, because it is not our business here to pass literary verdicts, but to measure the influence of the writers of the last century upon the men of to-day.

Now it is an indisputable fact that Stendhal has had, and still has, a profound influence upon later generations. Less vast and less animated than that of Balzac, perhaps inferior in talent and charm, his bold, dry work has, nevertheless, an unquestionable originality. It is impossible for us to read it without being moved in the mysterious and unexplored depths of our being. His genius goes neither high nor far, but he goes deep; and it is in the most secret recesses of our nature that he wields his narrow, yet all the more persistent, power.

And the frame of mind which Stendhal provokes is not difficult to determine. It may be summed up in a single word, a word much used nowadays, to which we should like to restore all its primitive moral vigour—wickedness.

Wickedness* is, obviously, the contrary of goodness. We know fairly well what goodness is in life, and we know that the finest work of the human mind is impregnated with it. The sincere love of our neighbour, care never to hurt him, an ardent desire to assuage the sufferings of others, the pain which another's misfortune gives us, pity for the weak, indulgence for the man who falls, forgiveness of injury, the thirst for justice, enthusiasm for all that is beautiful, the communion of our heart with the whole of humanity—are not these and other sentiments what we mean by "goodness"? And is it not in these virtues that, after a hundred years of experience, we recognise the indisputable nobleness of human nature? We have at least, in proof of it, the masterpieces of the poets, from Valmîki to Tolstoi, from Orpheus to Hugo. Goodness in the *Iliad* is Achilles shedding tears with the father of his vanquished enemy; in the *Odyssey* it is the profoundly human chant in which we see Menelaus and Helena reconciled on the threshold of age; in Sophocles it is the old men of Athens receiving Antigone and Œdipus; it is Socrates in the *Phædo;* it is the whole of Vergil with that trembling pity which extends even to the tears of things; it is Dante drawn to the very torments of his Francesca; it is Rabelais overflowing with indulgence and mercy; it is Balzac flinging into space, for all the disinherited of life, the last appeal of the divinised Séraphita; it is, from its mysterious sources lost in the mists of history to our own time, a great unbroken stream that flows on from age to age, ever broader and deeper, pouring into our eternal pain the eternal solace which Shakespeare called "the milk of human kindness."

There is one whose lips seem never to have touched this sacred milk which all great geniuses drink—Stendhal.

* See Note 4 (at end of volume).

Henri Beyle (*Stendhal*)

It is impossible to imagine a man and a work in which everything conspires more surely to produce the exact opposite of goodness.

First, the man. He was, in the full sense of the word, the very incarnation of egoism. He despised the humble —hated the powerful. He was at the same time a revolutionary as regards organised society and a reactionary as regards the " human scum," which he declared for ever incapable of sharing power. But in neither character had he any conviction or principle. It was a caprice, a whim, for the mere pleasure of being opposed to everybody else. It was the supreme joy of this charming man to irritate and contradict his fellows in everything that he said. An amiable nature! Did any-one praise the things of which he himself boasted? At once he changed his mind and set out to oppose the persons or things to which he had offered incense. There was in him some morbid craving for a furious opposition. He hated Napoleon while he was Emperor; as soon as Napoleon fell, he took to chanting his glory. To French he spoke evil of France; to Italians he insulted Italy.

Whence this incurable misanthropy? Broken illusions? Precocious suffering? Goodness imposed upon? Not in the least. He had always been the same. When a child, he detested his father; when a young man, he scorned his native land. He was born bad—that is all. He came into the world morally infirm. He brought the wickedness and egoism with him, as Cervantes brought heroism and generosity.

It is a fact that he burned with pride, or, rather, with a formidable vanity. Now, it is the quality of vanity to be insatiable, even on a throne. Stendhal had made his self the centre of the world. His megalomania took the form of hatred because men were clearly incapable

91

of doing him justice. In his own eyes he was the superior man, and, precisely because of his superiority, the world was bound to detest him. He returned the detestation with contempt. " Woe to the man who distinguishes himself," he says in *The Red and the Black*. And a little later he adds: " I have lived long enough to know that *difference engenders hatred.*"

Who can fail to see in these two propositions the double formula of the frame of mind—the ugliest frame of mind of all—which we may call wickedness from pride ? From this to awakening in us the instincts of brutal enjoyment, to unleashing the individual as a wild animal amidst a pack of other wild animals, is merely a matter of a little logic; and logic was Stendhal's supreme quality.

Did he follow his own doctrine to its last conclusion ? Probably not, because in that case he would never have written, but would have " lived finely," like Cartouche, Mandrin, Cæsar Borgia, the poisoner Lafargue, and some other heroes whose energy he praised. It was precisely because he lacked this " sublime energy " that he contented himself with singing its praises. Not being able to realise all the splendour of evil, he made his works resplendent with it.

However, his personal conduct is of little interest to us. We speak of his character only because his work is the reflection of it, and it is his work alone that matters; for it is that, not the life of the man, which has left traces of itself in humanity.

II

Now, his work has, morally, an admirable and a formidable unity. Here there is no hesitation or slow development; no contradiction in the conception of the world. Stendhal is consistent from one end to the other, and the ideas he inspires are always and everywhere the opposite of all that is generous and good.

All the heroes he flung into life, " all his world," as he used to say, are unscrupulous egoists, determined to do anything whatever to procure, at any cost, an hour of pleasure or power. For them existence has no other purpose than the satisfaction of all their desires. They have no ideal except the ardour of an over-excited passion. They are, naturally, like Stendhal himself, superior beings; they are endowed even beyond measure with all the faculties of genius. Shall I say that they are handsome and seductive ? More than that; they are beauty and seduction incarnate. They are fine, they are loved by women, they are envied and hated by the majority of men and served fanatically by a few. How can an obscure poor devil help but admire these magnificent creatures ? Yes, let us admire them, and wish to be in their place, and be drawn into their brilliant circle.

Young Fabrizio del Dongo, the hero of the *Chartreuse de Parme*, is adorned with every shining grace. He is chivalrous, enthusiastic, courageous, bold, tender, eloquent. What does he do with so many virtues ? He uses them solely in the pursuit of his passions from year to year, day to day, hour to hour. During his short career he does as much evil around him as it is physically possible to do; and he does it ingenuously, a smile upon his lips, innocent as a jaguar amongst gazelles. Then there is Count Mosca, the man of genius, the great politician. For the caprice of a woman he gambles with the kingdom confided to him; strews a few insignificant corpses here and there; robs the public treasury and betrays the State; then ends his edifying life in a peaceful retreat near Pompeii, surrounded by esteem and respect.

These are the best, the models ! If, by some chance,

the handsome young man was not born in a palace, and had not the love of duchesses and protection of the powerful for viaticum on his way to happiness, we have a still more magnificent hero, Stendhal's favourite hero, the beloved child of his genius, the ambitious and passionate plebeian, the wolf let loose in the social forest. We have Julien Sorel, one of the most finished types in French literature. But what a type! What gall!

The Red and the Black is Stendhal's masterpiece, perhaps the only work of his that will survive, certainly the work into which he has put his whole self, and which has most influence. In every enduring creative work the poet projects himself into his hero, and projects his hero into the reader. Hence that irresistible power of letters to which we refer constantly in these essays. And if, at first sight, the principle seems disputable as regards a Balzac or a Musset, it is quite indisputable in the case of Stendhal.

Julien Sorel is for Stendhal a powerful lens by means of which his concentrated rays burn and parch all that they touch. There is no other work so evidently desolating; and it is such by the sovereign will of its author. Sorel is the most finished incarnation of hatred; and he embodies it with so much genius that in the end he communicates the poison to us. Strange power of literary art! This envious and base creature, this hypocritical valet, this youthless calculator who begins by serving others in the hope that he will one day command, this plebeian who detests his family, despises his fellows, and hates all that is above him, this lackey dying because he cannot be an emperor, this badly emancipated slave dragging along all the rancour of the *ergastulum*, this unbridled and cunning blackguard, succeeds in the end in gaining our affection. We hang upon his fortunes, follow his adventures with beating hearts, suffer at his defeat, and weep over his death. Yes, we love him. We are with him against the whole world; or, rather, in the end it is he who lives in us.

It is because Stendhal has adorned his favourite hero with all the graces of his own mind. He has armed Sorel with his own ruthless logic, and by this he has made him all the more disturbing and dangerous.

By what subtle and all-embracing sophistry does Julien succeed in persuading himself and us that all his actions are legitimate? Even hypocrisy, the most hateful of vices, ends by taking on some air of heroism in this book. Julien cries:

> How fearfully difficult is this hypocrisy of every moment of life! It is enough to make pale the labours of Hercules. The Hercules of modern times is Sixtus V., deceiving for fifteen years in succession by his modesty forty cardinals who had seen the passion and pride of his youth.

And later, in a difficult pass, he calls to his aid " the genius of Tartufe."

How odious this Julien is; how vile and fundamentally ignoble; how we should despise him if we could examine him coolly! But can anyone examine the hero of a novel in cold blood? Can anyone escape the charm with which the author invests him? For Julien has all the luck. Instead of being punished for his hatred and pride, the author awards him what will seem to the sensitive reader the most radiant of crowns—an heroic and romantic death. After that, is it any use trying to prevent young and weak souls from admiring this particular specimen of humanity? Poets are responsible for their heroes. Stendhal's hero is, as far as my knowledge goes, the most pernicious of all, because he inspires misanthropy.

Not the glowing misanthropy of an Alcestis, angry at

the world because the reign of justice has not yet come. That misanthropy is, in the long run, but an excess of generosity. Alcestis does not hate humanity. On the contrary, he loves it even to pain; he is angry only because he does not find the race as beautiful as he had dreamed. Alcestis is the younger brother of Don Quixote. He would have set out to help men, but his brother has told him all his adventures, and he remains at home, impatient and agitated, furious that he cannot do good. Let some appeal ring out, and Alcestis will be off, like his elder brother, if it be only to fall upon windmills. Meantime he castigates men, because it pains him to see them wicked. It is the gesture of Jesus driving the traders from the Temple; to-morrow he will die to save them.

How different is the misanthropy of Stendhal and his Julien Sorel! How cold, deliberate, calculating! He sees only two sorts of men, dupers and duped; and, as the dupers are the elect, he takes his place resolutely with them. For the rest, he despises both classes: the dupers because they hinder his progress, the duped because they are fools. Stendhal asks:

What is conscience? Who appeals to the testimony of conscience if not the hypocrite who turns to fools in order to make dupes of them?

How far that is from the cry of Alcestis:

I hate all men, some because they are wicked and evil-doing, the others because they are complaisant to the wicked.

Listen, now, to the last monologue of Julien as he is about to die, in which he haughtily resumes his philosophic calm:

There is no such thing as a *natural right*. The word is nothing but a piece of ancient folly. . . . There is no *right* except where there is a law forbidding us to do a certain thing under threat of punishment. Before the law nothing is *natural* except the

96

strength of the lion and the need of the creature that is hungry, or is cold; *need*, in a word. . . . No, the people who are honoured are merely scoundrels who have had the good fortune never to have been caught red-handed. . . . Hypocrisy, or at least charlatanry, everywhere, even amongst the most virtuous and the greatest. . . . No, man cannot trust man.

Here it is man who is hated, and the hate is incurable.

What is likely to be the effect of such a theory, set in all the seduction of a captivating story, on the mind of young men ? There are few who do not in their youth have their fits of misanthropy: whether it be from disappointment at his own lot or disillusion as to the glamour of the world, the man who is entering life feels the accents of anger or indignation murmuring in him. At twenty one is always more or less Alcestis. And the higher one's powers are, the more one has to suffer. In that case one sees what ravages the creation of a Julien Sorel may make in strong imaginations. One easily conceives oneself equal to him in superior merit, and so one naturally becomes like him in his pride and his unbridled ambition. How many young men of generous soul I have myself known who have been disturbed by it throughout youth, sometimes throughout life !

In this deliberate corruption of characters we have— heavy as the word may seem—a real crime on the part of Stendhal.

III

Yes, I know. To talk about crime in connection with a work of art is to confess oneself a " simpleton." That is understood. Stendhal, in fact, was careful to let us know it himself. The malicious psychologist knew well the just indignation that his work would provoke, and he anticipated it by trying to make it ridiculous in advance. It is a trick that dates from the earthly paradise, but it always succeeds. Or, if it does fail anywhere, there is one country where its triumph is assured by ten centuries of experience—France.

Our land of physical bravery is remarkable for its intellectual cowardice. Here one is always sure of mastering people when one threatens them with sarcasm. The man who will die with arms in his hand will hesitate to hold an opinion that is not in fashion. Stendhal knew well how to profit by this pusillanimity. Listen to him in the Preface to his *Chartreuse* :

> But be careful ! This story is anything but moral; and now that you pride yourselves on your evangelical purity in France, it may draw upon you the epithet of murderer.

" Evangelical purity," eh ? How terrible ! "" I accused of evangelical purity ?" cries the good Frenchman. " I would rather die." And he joins Stendhal in his smile.

Elsewhere the author of *L'Amour* assures us that he does not write for the " flabby " public, the " sheep-like " public. He dedicates his *Chartreuse de Parme* to an initiated few, to a select public, or, as he calls it in an English phrase, to complete the distinction, " to the happy few." It is, of course, a *tribute to superiority ;* and that always succeeds in France.

" My book will be treated badly by the fools; only a few superior spirits will perceive its charm."

" The devil !" say the valorous Gauls at once; " let us perceive it." And the difficulty is not great.

Sooner or later, however, there come more stubborn souls upon whom the trick is wasted. One must then have the courage to tell the truth. In the whole of French literature Stendhal's work is the most conspicuous in having an influence that is opposed to every ideal. It is infinitely more unhealthy than that of Balzac, because it is unhealthy everywhere, always, indisputably, without the least tendency to good anywhere. Certainly Balzac created a deplorable frame of mind in fostering, by his seductive exaltation of the conquerors of life, the cult of success and of money; but, if he failed in his work, he did at least set before himself a magnificent task, and the short flights of his unfinished heroes bear witness that they wanted to rise toward the brightness of the sun.

Balzac's fault was to allow himself to be dazed by the pretentious splendour of social life, and to linger too long, with his fine men of ambition, over the material intoxications of the world. He sinned from weakness and lack of serenity. Stendhal, on the other hand, deliberately urges us to evil. He is disturbing and unhealthy of set purpose; he is so furiously; he has no other aim but that, until it becomes a sort of proud disinterestedness. He peers into the depths of our hearts for obscure instincts which we would not ourselves dare to discover. He stirs them with a fierce pleasure. He shakes them, and desperately enjoys seeing them rise to the surface. Listening to him, we are surprised and disturbed to find in ourselves things of which we were ignorant. Then, if we have a hesitating soul and a poorly tempered character, we begin to be astonished at the revelations that issue from our subconscious depths. We stand open-mouthed with vague admiration before the singular revealer, and we are ready to accept the direction which his deliberate philosophy would give us in regard to these larval instincts he reveals in us.

For the souls of men in our time it is plainly a disquieting symptom that such work should have fanatical admirers amongst us.

GEORGE SAND

She is woman, the feeble being, destined to represent the passions restrained or, if you prefer, suppressed by the laws; she is the will in conflict with necessity; she is love, bruising her blind front against all the obstacles set up by civilisation. . .
—Preface to *Indiana*.

CHAPTER V

GEORGE SAND

I

I AM really distressed to have to speak about George
Sand at the present moment [1903]. It looks as if
I were writing a topical article and joining in the assault
upon this poor woman whose worn linen has been shaken
by strong hands at every window of public curiosity. I
beg my readers, friendly or unfriendly, to understand at
once that I do not intend to say anything whatever about
the love-passages that the grand-niece of Marshal Maurice
de Saxe may or may not have experienced. Such a matter
is of no importance in a study of the influence her mind
has had.

What have we to do with these stories of a life that
has been placarded on every wall ? Whether George
Sand loved Peter or Paul, Chopin or Mérimée, Musset or
Pagello, the porter at the corner of the street or the lyre-
bearer, whether she was faithful for ten hours or ten years,
whether she did or did not make the moths that danced
round her captivating beauty suffer, does not in the least
affect the question of her fundamental character. These
personal anecdotes may arouse men's curiosity, but they
have nothing to do with the conflict of ideas.

The author of *Lélia*, we are told, loved love, and would
acknowledge no obstacle to the satisfaction of her passions.
Well, that is understood. She took pains to blazon it
to us by all the trumpets of her style. And now people
are anxious to prove to us that her conduct conformed

to her theories. It is only another proof that she was a woman of character.

Further, I consider that, in her adventure with Musset or any other of her lovers, all the advantages are on the side of George Sand. She acted consistently with her function as woman, which was to draw deeply moved souls within her orbit; and they were unfaithful to their duty as men, for that is to preserve tranquillity at heart. In this eternal duel which love is she brought off every victory with a high hand. She even infused into it a certain greatness of soul, for she was kind and indulgent to those she conquered. As to Musset, it is said that it made him a great poet; which will be considered later. At least, and beyond question, he showed himself a deplorable fool, and his whines do no honour to his sex.

I do not, therefore, begin this essay with any particular prejudice against George Sand. I am not setting out to avenge the " poor men " for the evil which this " monster of a woman " did them. So much the worse for them if they suffered; so much the better for her if she enjoyed their tears.

I confess that I have every sympathy with the author of *Lélia*, and I admire her magnificent development. She was nothing but desire and passion, it is said. Granted. But, lover for lover, I would rather have this strenuous and ardent poetess than all the affected and pretentious chatterers with their hypocritical whispers over the tea-table. She was, at all events, loyal and robust in the exactions of her heart and her senses. There is only a difference of degree between the sentimental woman of the lower middle class who yields to a few fops and a Messalina devouring men; and Messalina is the greater of the two. Really, they amuse me, these people who would settle the exact point at which the passions must stop if they are not to " pass the bounds." What compass do they use ? Is it not precisely the characteristic of passions to know no limit or restraint ? These surveyors of tempests remind me of children at the brink of the ocean trying to measure the height of the waves with crystal cups.

Let us put George Sand in her proper place; and in the scale of human glory it is a high place. She is a thousand cubits higher than all the women who went before her or have followed her. She is the great patroness, the undisputed " master," the archetype. The more I regard her, the more she seems to grow, until she reaches the proportions of a symbolical genius. And that is why she is so tremendously dark and unhealthy, for the spirit of which she is so powerful a synthesis is in itself fatally evil. It is the feminine spirit, or, to speak more precisely, the *female spirit*, as opposed to the *male spirit*. Just as Goethe, Rabelais, and Plato were, in the history of ideas, three of the most complete manifestations of the *male man*, the solar, bracing, creative man, so George Sand is the most superb incarnation of the *female woman*, the woman from whom issue shade, disturbance, and desolation.

I fear that in speaking thus I will offend at once the very few women who are likely to read me. Though I never write a single word with the intention of pleasing them, I should certainly not like to seem hostile to them, from any ironical humour or paradoxical spirit. I repeat here what I said in connection with Balzac: I have a horror of everything that looks like paradox or joke. If at times I chance to make my statements bluntly, or to infuse a little sarcasm into my discussion, it is because I so deeply love the truth that I would like to give it the swift and cauterising strength of a fiery sword. Let no one, therefore, see in this essay on George Sand the least inclination to refute, or even to discuss, what has been called " Feminism." Feminism is a political and social theory born, like all such theories, of claims that are, no doubt, legitimate, but are necessarily ephemeral. It is of no importance here to settle whether or no women have the right to vote, whether they ought to be cyclists, painters, or lawyers, and whether it is possible for them to produce large works just as well as the bipeds of the opposite sex. For my part I see no reason why all the women of the middle class should not be novelists, and all the women of the world lyric poets. Those are details of morals or fashion which have for me only an accidental interest. I would raise my subject to a different and higher region. . For, even if all women were " exquisite writers " and all men imbeciles—even if chatterers in petticoats took the place of phrase-makers in trousers in our Parliaments—there would still be in the world two spirits eternally attracting each other and eternally conflicting, the perpetual shock of which gives life to the entire human epic: the *male* spirit and the *female* spirit, or, if one prefers a less exact but less blunt word, the *feminine* spirit. And all the transitory theories of men would, even if they had an absolute unanimity of mortals on their side, not cause the fundamental laws of life to swerve by one hair's breadth.

II

Let us go back, if you will, to the origin of the world; and keep calm, for we shall very quickly get as far as the Deluge. But the subject is so important that it is worth while tracing it to its remotest source. Have you ever asked yourself why all the prehistoric legends of the most different races made woman a sort of fatal calamity to

which man had to submit ? You know the legend of an
earthly paradise, and also that of Pandora, the wife of
Epimetheus. By what strange adventure have the
luminous genius of the Greeks and the sombre genius of
the Semites come to this agreement in their symbol
of the pernicious feminine power ?

Listen, on the one hand, to the fierce Ecclesiastes:

And I find more bitter than death the woman, whose heart is
snares and nets, and her hands as bands.

On the other hand, hear the sunny Hesiod:

An equal wonder seized gods and men as soon as they saw
this fatal marvel, so injurious to mortals; for from this virgin
[Pandora] came the race of women with full breasts, those dangerous women, a cruel scourge, living amongst men.

I spare you quotations from the Egyptians, Hindus,
Persians, and Chinese. They agree in showing us the
sages of all ages and countries appalled at what Ecclesiasticus calls " the malice of woman."

The Feminist leaders reply to this unanimous testimony
of the ancients that men are tyrannical and cruel. They
say that from the beginning of time until our own day
the conduct of man toward woman was, with few exceptions, that of cave-man: that is to say, the absolute
domination of a powerful and brutal being over a frail
and tender being. If at times, they say, the weaker
creature used her charms to overcome the strong and
make him carry out her whims, it was simply because,
being a slave, she was compelled to use trickery and lies
in order to evade the despotism of the master.

This theory is simple and ingenuous; it has the advan-
tage of not being above the heads of humble folk. Unfortunately, it explains nothing at all, and it is completely
at variance, not only with the traditions and legends of
distant peoples, but also with the precise words of the

ancient thinkers. History shows rather that, from the moment civilised humanity began to mutter a few general ideas, man has never ceased to complain bitterly of the evil that came to him from woman. All the legends and all the theogonies bear witness to it. The symbol of Maia, of Eve, and of Pandora, the Venus Victrix of the Greeks, the Astarte of the Tyrians, the Isis of Egypt, give us so many poetic demonstrations of it.

If we wish to take no notice of the eloquence of sacred myths, let us consider the words of men; let us read the primitive poets. Is it not true that in all their works we seem to find some obscure dread of woman? They feel themselves vanquished in advance by the mysterious power which she has in her, and, according to race and temperament, either they submit resignedly to this messenger of fate or they pour bitter invectives upon her.

On an earlier page we gave two characteristic phrases, one from Ecclesiastes and one from Hesiod. Would you like to turn to the *Iliad* and all the poems of the Homeric cycle? What a symbol of the feminine power there is in Helen, the cause of so much war and sorrow!

> To suffer so many evils for such a woman!

cry the ancient Trojans. And they resign themselves to it with the quiet patience which the Hellenic poet ascribes to them.

Others, however, are less resigned when they suffer so many evils, and they growl like wounded beasts. Listen to the plaint of old Jesus ben Sirach, the author of Ecclesiasticus :

> Go not after woman in quest of love,
> For fear thou fall into the net;
> Look not curiously upon a maid,
> Lest thou be caught by her charms;

> From the beautiful woman turn away thine eye
> And dwell not on a strange beauty.
> How many have wandered astray on account of woman,
> From whom desire shoots like fire.

And later this pitiful cry, the cry of one vanquished without revolt and without hope:

> Better the wickedness of man than the goodness of woman !

So much for the brutal cave-men ! What do you, imperturbable philosophers, think of them ? Are these the triumphant cries by which a victor usually announces his undisputed domination ? A nice conqueror, indeed, this eternal grumbler, who seems to shudder with terror at the least gesture of his captive !

And this terror, the foundation of ancient wisdom, which we catch, shuddering, in the first mutterings of thinking humanity, rolls from age to age, literature to literature, civilisation to civilisation. It is that which makes the heroic Ulysses flee Calypso's island and the shores on which the sirens sing. It is that which drives Æneas, the founder of empires, far from the shore where the intoxicating Dido weeps; it is that which binds Samson in the palace of the Philistines; it is that which holds Hannibal's army in the delights of Capua; it is that which causes the panic of Antony's soldiers; it is that which drives the mystic Christians into the solitude of the desert, and makes the studious disciples of St. Benedict seek inviolable retreats on the tops of the mountains; it is, in fine, that which, repeated from age to age, breaks out in the work of the most modern poets, and inspires Alfred de Vigny with lines that seem to have been taken from the legendary Bibles:

> Companion ever near, whose heart's so far from sure,
> Woman, the sickly child, a dozen times impure.

What, is Vigny also—the beautiful Vigny, model of all nobleness, purest soul of poet-cavaliers—is he also a cave-man? Were the great hermits, who went to the depths of the Thebaid to flee the danger of the feminine mystery, cave-men? And the Greeks, and the Romans, and the Hebrews, and the Egyptians, and all the sages of all wisdoms, from Homer to Vergil, from Ecclesiastes to Plato, were they all strong men unscrupulously crushing frail creatures for the mere pleasure of dominating them?

Who can fail to see that, on the contrary, from the beginning of the world it was almost always the woman who triumphed over the man? Or, rather—and here we come to the higher truth—it was the *female spirit* that often triumphed over the *male spirit;* and it is the struggle between these two spirits that gives a tragic grandeur to the story of man.

Let us follow this struggle of the two eternal elements along the course of human evolution, and we shall see that the perpetual conflict of man and woman, of which feminism is one of the ephemeral forms, corresponds to another vast conflict which goes on uninterruptedly from the atom to the star. Let us try to settle in what the male spirit and the feminine spirit consist, and perhaps we shall discover there the whole problem of civilisation. Then, by means of this large detour, we shall understand why the work of a woman of genius, a woman so energetically and absolutely woman as George Sand was, cannot, from its very nature, be other than an unhealthy work, a work of disturbance, disorder, and impure sadness.

III

If it were not too pretentious, and especially too long, to go back to the origin of things in discussing a few works of romance, it would be interesting to see in the conflict of the male spirit and the female spirit the fundamental law of the universe. Everywhere we find two principles eternally present: a principle of repulsion, which imparts an indefinite movement to every atom and every globe, and a principle of attraction, which keeps all these atoms and globes near each other, and forces them to form systems. The world-system results from the balance of these two principles. Whence do they both come? There the great mystery begins, and the mind of man frets and fumes on the threshold of that mystery age after age. Materialistic or spiritualistic, all our philosophies seek only to discover, to divine, to feel the first cause, for ever unknown. But, while the cause is hidden, the law has been formulated definitively for us. We know not the why of things, but we know the how.

We do not know the primary reason why the earth goes round the sun, but we have, on the basis of unchanging facts, calculated the precise features of this invariable revolution. It is the same with human evolution, or, rather, revolution. From the most distant ages this has shown two principles confronting each other: one that seems to have the mission to create, to fertilise, unceasingly to organise life, and one whose visible function it is to draw to itself every passing germ of life, to attach itself thereto with a blind ardour, to make it constantly begin anew the same cycle round itself. The first principle is active, the second passive. The first is the male principle, the second the female principle. Our science does not know the first cause of these human laws, any more than it does in the case of the cosmic laws. But, although it is impossible for us to settle the formula of these social evolutions with the same exactness as Newton formulated the rhythm of cosmic revolutions, we are in a position to consider so long a stretch of the history of the earth that we are able to follow and measure the masculine and feminine principles in their constant relations.

What does the first represent in humanity ? The desire to create and, consequently, to change: the unceasing search for a more harmonious and better-arranged life; the substitution of conscious and rhythmic will for the blindness and disorder of nature—in two words, the spirit of *social evolution*.

What does the second represent ? Passive receptivity: the irresistible craving to perpetuate the species; the instinct of recommencement; the obscure law of the earth which urges to absorb and reproduce unceasingly with the same unconscious passion—in two words, the spirit of *natural conservation*.

The first principle corresponds, in the celestial order, to the movement which animates worlds: the other corresponds to the attraction which draws them to each other. The first is the principle of *action*, the second the principle of *love*.

Which is the better, the masculine or the feminine principle ? These are quite childish quarrels about precedence. It would be just as sensible to ask whether the centrifugal or the centripetal force is the more important. Both principles are equally necessary for the development of civilisation; and just as, in the astral system, any disturbance of equilibrium would entail frightful disorder, so in humanity, whenever the male spirit comes to preponderate over the female spirit, or the female spirit over the male spirit, there is a cataclysm or a dissolution.

Certainly at this particular hour of eternity when our race makes its appearance on the planet Earth we see the stars move in an unchanging order on the plains of heaven, and we imagine that this marvellous celestial equilibrium, the beautiful rhythm of which extorts our admiration, has never been, and can never be, disturbed. But how do we know ? Who can say that in the millions of ages that have preceded this imperceptible minute in which we pass, these worlds have not been disturbed and shaken by formidable conflicts of opposing forces ? Who can say that in the vast field of immensity there have not been terrible and gigantic events ? Who knows what combats the suns may have sustained before they came to group themselves in the harmonious order of the constellations ?*

By analogy we can formulate, almost in mathematical terms, the law of the relations between the masculine and the feminine spirit and indicate their reciprocal influence on human evolution.

Suppose there were some disturbance of equilibrium in the rhythm of the heavenly bodies. What would happen ? Our intuition can easily perceive it. If the force which animates the stars prevailed over attraction, all the globes would fly in disorder across the heavens in a fantastic whirl, and there would inevitably be a shock the mere thought of which makes us shudder. If, on the other hand, the force of attraction became preponderant, the stars would gradually slow down, would cease to resist, and would in the end fall weakly into each other, thus effecting a supreme unification which would be like death.

In the first case it would be chaos; in the second, annihilation. Between the two are harmony and beauty.

* In point of fact, we have every reason to know that the ordered family of the solar system has issued out of a vast conflict between the members of a far more numerous and disorderly family; and this probably applies to the stars of the stellar system.—TRANSLATOR.

H

We do not see—rather, we no longer see—this conflict in the cosmic system, but we find it unceasingly in the human system from the apparent beginning of civilisation to the hour in which we live. The two principles, male and female, action and love, have always been at war; and it is only in the rare periods when there has been equilibrium between them that, for the glory of the earth, those magnificent civilisations have flourished by which our imagination is still stirred and illumined.

Hence the following law, which the whole of history is ready to confirm by experience:

Whenever the male spirit prevails over the feminine spirit, there is violence, despotism, abuse of power, and *barbarism*.

Whenever the masculine spirit and the feminine spirit have approximately equal influence, there is splendour, prosperity, and a complete development of *civilised life*.

Whenever the feminine spirit prevails over the masculine, there is arrest, decomposition, and *decadence*.

IV

What a stirring, rich, splendid epic one could write if one were to trace through the whole course of terrestrial life the dramatic struggle of the male spirit and the female spirit! How many obscurities of our destiny would be lit up in that light! But I leave it to the reader to imagine this eternal conflict for himself, merely drawing such attention to it that he may realise its tragic grandeur.

Does the male spirit triumph? Then see the march of the fierce crushers of races, the proclaimers of brutal energy, the dreamers of universal empire, all the crude missionaries of action, in whom action, beneficent as it is in itself, becomes maleficent by its very excess. Behold the Nimrods, the Nabuchodonosors, the Cambyses, the Cyruses, the Alexanders, the Cæsars, the Attilas, the William the Bastards, Simon de Montfort, Charles of Anjou, Charles V., the Napoleons, and all those other bloody and terrible males who, exalting force at the expense of love, shifted the axis of human equilibrium and hurled chaos into the historical evolution.

On the other hand, does the feminine spirit gain the predominance ? Then see the dreadful fall of Memphis and of Babylon; Troy delivered to the flames because it received into its palace the fatal smile of Helen; expiring Corinth and Capua, Carthage and Athens; Alexandria handed over to the victorious Cæsars; Rome, enervated by four centuries of imperial pleasure, falling before the assault of Genseric; Byzantium and its long agony; the dawning glory of Occitania, where courts of love celebrate the triumph of Woman, crumbling, defenceless and nerveless, under the strong sword of the northern barbarians; the . . .

Let us break off this dangerous list. We should be compelled by the very march of history to whisper names which are dear to us.

In what form does masculine wickedness reveal itself ? In the exaggerated triumph of strength. What form does feminine wickedness take ? The exaggerated triumph of love. Must we conclude that strength and love are accursed things ? No. It is impossible to say whether the masculine or the feminine spirit is the more hurtful. Each in turn is responsible for grave things that have been done by men. But there is a radical difference between them, and in the light of this we may set right the misunderstandings which for more than ten thousand years have inspired male writers with their legendary maledictions of woman.

It is that, of the two spirits, masculine and feminine, the

one is easy to measure, but to define the other is impossible. The one is visible, even blatant: the other dark and mysterious. Whatever danger threatens civilisation from the exaggeration of strength, we have some chance of defending ourselves against it. Nimrod or Attila may have thousands of swords and lances at his command, but we can count them, and, even when they crush us, we know why.

The feminine spirit, on the other hand, entirely escapes our vigilance. We do not know that it lies in wait for us. It hovers about us when we least expect it. It enters noiselessly the most tranquil of lives and the most prosperous of civilisations. It is as intangible as the night-breezes. One would almost say that it issues from the earth itself, a treacherous and disturbing soul whose evil is never perceived until it is too late.

Hence the strange terror exhibited amongst all races and in all literatures in regard to *woman's malice*. " The woman more bitter than death, whose heart is snares and nets, and her hands as bands," says Ecclesiastes. To which the gentle Vergil adds, " Varium et mutabile semper," and Shakespeare his " Perversity, thy name is woman." And in our own time Proudhon ends with this expression of terrified anger: " Woman is the desolation of the just man."

One could make large volumes—I believe that such have been published—merely by collecting the most famous quotations of ancient and modern writers on the "perfidy of woman," adding the popular proverbs in which whole nations have given expression to this universal misogyny.

Are not all these words—malice, perfidy, perversity, restlessness, desolation, etc.—just a proof that the power of woman is obscure and unintelligible, and that man has always been angry because he must submit to it without being able to combat it, unless he resigns himself to it with bitterness ?

What is it, then, this mysterious and invincible power ? Is it so invisible that we cannot grasp it, so mysterious that we cannot determine its law ? It is a well-known power, and it is waste of time to seek new words for it. It is love, and nothing else. It is the instinctive craving of the woman to love, and, consequently, the natural tendency to make others love her. The whole danger of civilisation comes from that. Just as man is by nature wholly creation and movement, so woman is wholly love and desire. Her unchanging destiny is to draw men to her; the race would not survive were it not for this sexual attraction. Blind as a force of the earth, the force of love is necessarily unconscious, and therefore passionate. And it is as well that this should be so, for, if woman were able to discuss and reason upon her love, she would at once renounce it because of the pain it will bring later.

On the other hand, this love, which is for woman the paramount preoccupation of life, must be for man only a necessary and natural function that must never wholly absorb him. His work is vast enough to give him the right, or to impose upon him the duty, of assigning only certain moments of the day to the act of love.

He has the field to conquer and sow, the road to make, the herd to guide, the house to build, order to maintain in the tribe, and, later, cities and nations to organise. Meantime the family grows, thanks to the warm and ever vigilant love of the spouse and mother; and women begin again to love, and men to act.

After passing through the slavery of an inevitable barbarism, during which the masculine spirit predominates over the feminine spirit, a day arrives when woman becomes what she ought to be: the companion and equal of man in that untroubled association, the harmony of which, perfectly secured, maintains the peace of prosperous families and sustains the grandeur of civilisations.

But it is the nature of every force to tend to excess. Just as in the age of barbarism the male spirit made too much of action and despised love, so, as soon as the balance is restored, the female spirit tends to make too much of love and to prevail over masculine action. Compelled to love unceasingly, woman conceives love to be the higher mission of humanity. As soon as man has become, instead of her master, as he was, her companion and friend, she has but one dream—to make him love her as ardently as she loves him. Hence all the seductions, often perfectly innocent seductions, which the classic poets justly called " the wiles of woman." And the balance is disturbed once more. The masculine spirit, without distrust at first of the unconscious and natural malice of the feminine spirit, abandons itself gradually to the charm which surrounds it. Man ends, like woman, in thinking always of love and seeing in it, not a function, but the whole aim of life; and from that moment the victory of woman is assured.

As soon as the love-passion has entered the heart of a man, that man is lost for action. It is impossible for him to be an organiser or a creator, for he has lost serenity, the attribute of virile strength. Similarly, when this kind of love becomes the predominant motive of social life, when men and women are equally obsessed by it, when, instead of being hidden away as a dark and terrestrial function, it exalts itself to the degree of divinity, and proclaims itself king of the world, then, be sure, civilisation is tainted in its vital forces. The worm is in the fruit. The fall is inevitable. Slowly or quickly, death is on the way.

That is why all the great leaders of peoples and souls, from Moses and Orpheus to the severe thinkers of the last century, have instinctively combated the feminine spirit, and have stigmatised woman as the predestined enemy of the hero and the fatal destroyer of nations. But it was not woman they should have commended to the distrust of men. It was love, with which woman is possessed, and against which we must be on our guard.

V

Woe to any civilisation in which love becomes the leading motive of life and the most important theme of literature. Woe to any race in which the feminine spirit has triumphed over the masculine spirit.

Yet we are amongst these races and civilisations: not only France, but the whole Latin race, and perhaps the whole of Europe, if not, presently, the whole of humanity. It is because I perceived this that I undertook to write these essays against those whom I call " bad masters ": those who are dominated and disturbed by the feminine spirit, and who have passed on to us their disturbance and degeneration.

It seems to me that it is not now necessary to insist at any length on the particular case of George Sand, or, for the same reason, on any of the women poets and novelists, of whom she is the highest and most glorious.

Her work is bad, fundamentally and thoroughly bad, because from one end to the other it is an exaltation, an apotheosis, of love.

Quotations ? Proofs ? It is needless. I should have to quote the whole of her work. It is the very principle of her work that is pernicious. It is enough to read one page of her to gather from what I have said the inevitable conclusion to which I have been leading.

Listen just to these synthetic lines which summarise so eloquently her whole conception of love and life:

Indiana is a type. She is woman, the feeble being, destined to represent the passions restrained or, if you prefer, suppressed by the laws; she is the will in conflict with necessity; *she is love, bruising her blind front against all the obstacles set up by civilisation.*

What an admirable, symbolical, definite expression of the feminine defence ! What sober and forceful eloquence ! How the whole exasperated individualism of woman finds vigorous expression in these few words ! "Passions suppressed by the laws"—is this not the eternal cry of independence raised by the spirit of nature against the order and rhythm of society, whose higher mathematics angers and humiliates the disorder of obscure things ? "The will in conflict with necessity"—is this not the whole egoism in revolt of the being who has made herself the centre of the world, and who admits no need of an organisation apart from her own desires ? And this sublime and fiercely sincere formula, "Love bruising her blind front against all the obstacles of civilisation." How beautiful ! What a revelation of the genius of woman in the simple mingling of these figures of speech ! How clear it is that no man could ever have spoken with this accent !

Yes, love has *a blind front*, and that is just why it has to be chained, like a slave whose revolts are dangerous; for, the moment he is free, he will rend everything about him, and will bruise himself against what George Sand calls, with so feminine a candour, *the obstacles of civilisation.*

It is for the purpose of extolling this blind love that

George Sand wrote all her works. It is against these obstacles, hated by every woman who is really a woman, that she has uttered her impulsive war-cry. Read *Lélia*, *Indiana*, *Mademoiselle La Quintinie*, and the *Lettres d'un voyageur*—read the whole of her works—and you will find everywhere the struggle of *passions* against *laws*, the revolt of nature against society, the insurgency of the earth against the sun, the proclamation of the triumph of the female spirit.

What evil have not such works done! What a germ of social destruction lives in them! Posterity alone will be able to appreciate the disasters. We are ourselves so much tossed in the vortex that we have ended by growing accustomed to it. And the work is continued by the ever-growing army of women writers.

But is George Sand the first to incur the charge? The feminine spirit had long taken possession of literature and of minds everywhere. It was men who were the first to proclaim their weakness. And as soon as love had been enthroned as the god of life, it was proper that its natural priestesses should claim the right to conduct the cult. For my part, I admit that George Sand and all the other women who write amorous works are quite true to their function. I have more sympathy with them than with Rousseau and Chateaubriand, Benjamin Constant, Musset, Baudelaire, or any other of the lamentable poets of passion. It would be unjust and childish to throw all the blame upon the women writers. They have done no worse than the majority of their colleagues of male aspect. If they have the greater part in the degeneration of our souls, and the unrest of our hearts, one must at least recognise, in their defence, that they merely obey their innate tendencies; and that it is our foolish complaisance, and, still more, our deplorable example which have encouraged in them the literary development of their amorous instincts.

Must we bow our heads, accept the evil without a word, and await the final decomposition without a struggle? Surely we can put greater trust than this in virile energy To yield would be cowardice: to despair, mere feebleness of spirit. As long as a civilisation is alive, there is a chance of recovery. However decrepit our literature may be, it may recover its youth. We must create masculine works, a masculine art, a masculine thought; we must make our souls and minds masculine once more; we must awaken. It is there that we shall have the real struggle between the masculine and the feminine spirit, not in a miserable rivalry in the bookshops.

Let us deliver ourselves and our readers from the amorous prejudice. Let us make a serene and robust youth. Let us guard the future against woman's philtre. Do not let us tear up the work of George Sand and her 3,000 disciples. What would be the good of it? You cannot suppress what exists. You must fight the danger with equal weapons. But let us bring out sunny-minded works which will, by their luminous influence, dissipate the morbid temptations that have for more than a hundred years been put into the souls of the young by the disturbing works of women and their slaves. The task will not be without risks. The feminine spirit will not idly suffer itself to be driven from its vast empire. They who make the attempt must expect the enmity of the world, in which woman rules despotically. But what does it matter? There are other glories than those of the battlefield, other heroisms than that of facing death.

ALFRED DE MUSSET

The greatest of evils is sadness of heart.—Ecclus. xix. 18.

CHAPTER VI

ALFRED DE MUSSET

I

I WILL not waste time in discussing the position which ought to be assigned to Musset amongst the poets of the nineteenth century. This mania for assigning their hierarchic rank to writers has too long been one of our most widespread puerilities. Was Musset as great a poet as Hugo, Lamartine, or Baudelaire ? Not as great ? The third poet of the century ? The fifth ? The seventh ? These are innocent little games that we will leave to college folk. Only one thing matters—was he a genius ? In other words, did he create a living work, and has this work left its mark on the minds of men ? It is beyond question.

I do not think any other mortal who ever came into the world to write poetry had so large a number of charming fairies round his cradle. His genius included all the graces and all the seductive arts. Above all, he received that gift of harmonious phrase which makes his style as captivating and irresistible as the rustle of leaves or the murmur of waves. He received that gift of imagery in virtue of which each of his thoughts takes external form in a luminous reflection. He received that gift of lyricism by means of which his soul enfolds us, raises us, and bears us away with it across space, like Faust's cloak, which he invoked. He received the gift of emotion, of tenderness, and of pity, which makes his every verse groan, weep, and pour out like the little waterfalls which tremble and leap in the forest. He received, in fine, a supreme treasure, a solid classical education which taught him all the secrets of eternal art, and the science of using well his other gifts.

So that at the age of twenty, handsome as a young god, fresh as a hero, loved like a bringer of good news, he was radiant with genius and hope; and he inspired such confidence that, upon his first flight, he was greeted as the long-expected poet.

Unfortunately, it was just this brilliant precociousness that enfeebled the spring of his genius, and condemned Musset to play the part of an incurable spoiled child. Was it because he knew nothing of those hard struggles which temper character ? Because he had not to experience the bracing trial of obscure isolation and patient poverty ? I do not know; but the fact remains that he never ripened, and that the splendid flower which opened so suddenly, wet with dew, one spring morning, shrivelled on its stalk without ever producing the golden fruit that was expected. Musset had the misfortune to break out in full glory at the age of twenty; and he was doomed to remain a poet of twenty all his life. And as, after his twentieth year, he knew only tender outpours and delicious mistakes, he would sustain as long as possible that which had excited at once the pleasure of his body, the emotions of his heart, and the rise of his young glory— love. Therefore he made love the one inspiration of his life and his work.

What sort of love ? This great lyre-bearer chose no other part in the world but to sing of the caprices of working girls and the sentimentalities of students. When the breath of his genius moves him to proclaim his poetic mission, these are the only cries he has :

> What's life or death to me, my Muse ?   I love
> And will grow pale.   I love, and I will mourn,
> And give my genius for one well-bought kiss.

* * * * *

> Ay, and for ever I would blazon forth
> This thing—that, having sworn to let love go,
> I have sworn again to live and die for love.*

And this profession of poetic faith, made amidst the triumphs of his twenty-fifth year, he will mutter again when, prematurely aged, he feels the painful end coming:

> If two names must perforce stir the chords of my lyre,
> They shall be but the names of Ninette and Ninon.

A high destiny, indeed, for a man of such parts! No doubt it was that he might play this part of gondolier, of guitarist, of cavalier, that the whole race worked in preparation for the birth of the poet.

If at least the great predestined had kept some masculine dignity in his fall—if he had praised the living joy of love and, like some fawn in heat in the depths of the forest, had uttered cries of conquest and possession—he would still have the pride of a little strength, however far below the level of his genius, and, in default of moral energy, he would none the less inspire a sentiment of virility.

No. His work is one sustained groan. He renounces the idea of victory. Love has become in him so sickly and perverse an obsession that he mingles it with all the acts of his life and all the interests of his age.

II

I know nothing more astounding in this regard than his famous *Letter to Lamartine*. One poet writes to another, both of them distinguished. They live in the dawn of an age when the whole race is being transformed. They have been witnesses of prodigious adventures. And the only question that occupies the mind of the

* From the translation by W. H. Pollock, *An August Night.*

127

young poet at the height of his power is, why women push wickedness to the extent of abandoning their unhappy lovers:

> From these lines, gracious poet, learn the truth that I love.

And as the love has not been happy, the confidence at once proceeds:

> Shall I dare what I felt in that hour of distress,
> Breathe into thy grave ear, and confide my lament ?
> In what words could I tell what no words can express ?

He dares, nevertheless, and here is the ground of the pain which " no words can express ":

> Such was I, left forlorn by my light, faithless love.
> For the first time I felt in me sorrow's fierce smart,
> As if some bloody shaft through my being it drove;
> And I sat far from men, in the night of my heart.

And Musset tells Lamartine that the " faithless love " was so cruel as to leave him " at carnival time ":

> Oh my God ! Weep alone through so sombre a night !
> My one love, what dark evil had I done to you
> You should break the fair troth you had sworn in God's sight,
> I might hold you the light of my life, so Heaven knew ?

It is so frightful a disaster that it moves the young poet to apostrophise his illustrious predecessor thus:

> O thou who wert wise in the love of Elvire,
> Can two mortals thus part with a lasting good-bye ?
> Can one write that fell word without trembling or fear ?
> Can the heart or the lips frame a message so drear ?—
> The red lips which a kiss had united for aye.
> Can thy love understand how a bond in the soul,
> Growing stronger each day, in the home or the mart,
> Till the flag of revolt the proud will doth unroll,
> Till its fabric be one with the web of the heart;—
> Canst thou grasp how this bond that ten years had held fast,
> Held so fast for ten years that our lives one life seemed,
> Should thus suddenly break, leave our hearts overcast,
> And us full of amaze at the bliss we had dreamed ?

No, it is quite unintelligible; and Musset concludes:

> Back to heaven flies the soul when we lose those we love;
> Here on earth 'tis a pale living corpse that remains,
> The dark home of despair, loth to linger above.

Certainly Musset deserved to be " treated as a child ";
of which he complains in a famous sonnet.

Another example. Let us take his *Hope in God*, the
most elevated piece he ever attempted to write, the piece
which best shows the native nobleness of his soul. Even
in this poem, where at times we seem to catch the strong
spirit of Pascal, even in this flight toward " the infinite
which torments us," the young poet cannot forget love:

> Would I have all that man in his vastest desires,
> All that heart in its hungriest moments requires,
> Grant me power, grant me health, grant of wealth an increase,
> *Grant me love, the one flower on this desolate ball.*
> May the sweet blonde Astarte, beloved of old Greece,
> Open-armed from her isle come to answer my call !

" The one flower on this desolate ball!" This is not
one of those phrases which the frivolous epicureans of the
seventeenth and eighteenth centuries penned with a
smile. It is the deep and agitated cry of a sincere soul;
and it is just at the moment when he kneels before God,
in whom he believes and hopes, it is in this solemn, almost
sacred, hour that he insists that the only happiness
in life is to see the blonde Astarte open her arms to
him !

What are we to expect, then, in those poems of his
which were solely inspired by love, such as *The Nights*, his
masterpiece ? They breathe nothing, they vibrate and
tremble with nothing, but love ? History, nature, heaven,
even the gods—everything turns in maddening appeals
round this single fact that the poet has been deceived
by his lover.

> But thou shalt hear it; take thy lyre, my Muse,
> And let my memory speak to its sweet chords.
>
> *   *   *   *   *
>
> When, in the evening's light, beside the brook
> We walked together on the silvered grass,
> Where the white spectral aspen marked our path,
> And the cloud-haunted moon sent trembling rays
> To give us fitful guidance; when these arms—
> O God! I see it all! Let me forget it!
> I guessed not then the goal of all my hopes,
> But wrathful Fate must have been poor of prey
> When it looked down and fixed its gaze on me,
> And plagued me thus for seeking happiness.
>
> W. H. POLLOCK.

Musset tells the Muse in all its horrible details, this misfortune inflicted upon him by the anger of the jealous gods:

> Thou, Muse, shalt hear an unimpassioned tale
> Of all my weary dreams and bitter madness.
> I'll tell the time, the occasion, and the place.
> How I remember! 'Twas an autumn night . . .
>
> W. H. POLLOCK.

We know the rest. What young man in France, or elsewhere, has not learned by heart these trembling and burning lines which tell of the cruelty of a "faithless woman" with so much poetic eloquence that one cannot help being moved to tears by the poet's lament, and forget as a rule how petty is the cause of all the disturbance? At last his anger breaks forth, and anathemas succeed groans:

> Oh, shame on her who taught me truth could die!
> Shame on thee, woman of the sombre glance,
> Whose fatal love o'ershadows all my youth!
>
> W. H. POLLOCK.

He has, in truth, "lost his reason," as he says, for, when he would pass from anger to forgetfulness, he will have nothing less than the protection of the whole universe to help him to accomplish this heroic deed :

                    Hearken then,
My goddess, and record this solemn vow:
By the blue vault of yonder gracious heaven;
By the bright sphere that borrows Venus' name,
And pearl-like trembles in the far-off sky;
By nature's grandeur and almighty love;
By the firm star that is the sailor's guide;
By all the meadows, all the woods and groves;
By life's omnipotence—ay, by the pith
That doth invigorate the universe,
I banish thee for ever from my mind—
Wreck of a maddening and insensate love,
Dead memory of a bygone tale of woe !
                              W. H. POLLOCK.

I have quoted this tirade in full because it is characteristic. It is difficult to heap up so much eloquence, so much lyricism, for the mere purpose of expressing the vanity of an inconstant soul and the unconscious egoism of a childish heart. So many terrible vows before one can forget a rather flighty lover ! The whole of human pain invoked because a sensitive student has been crossed in love !

III

His admirers reply:

It is just this invocation of pain that makes Musset's work great and pure. He was not merely the poet of love; he was also the poet of pain, and it is here that he is profound and sublime. It matters little that the cause of the pain was slight, and seems to us inadequate. If the pain is sincere, if the poet has really suffered, it is all that we require for his sobs to move us and awaken in us a noble sympathy. He has become, through his own suffering, a magnificent interpreter of ours; and as everybody in this world suffers, all ought to be grateful to Musset for lending his sonorous voice to our common sorrows, and all ought to exclaim with him:

A great sorrow alone makes the heart of man great !

That is what they say, and write, and teach. Well, it is false. It is a fallacy of the heart. It is a suggestion made by our flattered weakness. It is not true that pain suffices to make us great; or, rather, it is not true that every sorrow is a great sorrow. It is not enough to weep over anything whatever, or about anything whatever, to make the tears noble and generous. It is not true that all cries of despair are beautiful and all sobs are tragic, even in spite of their sincerity and their communicative emotion. The sublime in our pain is not measured by its intensity; it is proportioned to the greatness of the cause.

Which of us has not seen sensitive and nervous persons weep frantically and wring their hands in profound despair at the least contravention of their will ? Who has not heard ailing old men or spoiled children turn the world upside down because some caprice of theirs was thwarted ? Who has not known women of great charm curse life and let genuine tears stream from their eyes because they had " nothing to put on," or they were not allowed to go to a dance ?

Why, only yesterday, as I was writing the preceding pages in a room that opened on the Bay of Naples,* opposite the hills of Sorrento, I heard somewhere near the cries of a child. And the sobs that came from his heart had so penetrating and so moving a rhythm that, forced into sympathy, I left my work to go and console the unhappy child. It was the son of a neighbour, a delightful golden-haired boy, French like myself; and his blue eyes were full of tears. His parents had gone out, leaving him in charge of an old nurse, and he was playing on a terrace that overlooked the sea. I ran. I took him in my arms, and asked him the cause of his trouble. His little frame was so shaken with grief that he could not speak. In turn he pointed to the terrible waves, in which some

* See Note 5 (at end of volume).

atrocious drama had been perpetrated, and to heaven, which he invoked with uplifted arms. At last the sobs died down, the gentle voice could mutter a few words, and, under my reassuring caresses, the child gave me the story of the frightful event: his doll had fallen into the sea !

I could not help but think immediately of the " great sorrows " of Alfred de Musset.

We hear a gentle voice in accents of lament, we see a young and charming person pointing with desperate gestures to heaven, we are shaken in every fibre by an irresistible rhythm of genuine sobs; and what is it all about ? We hear the whole story. He invokes God and the gods. He calls to his aid the whole of the race, the whole of nature. He swears that he is crushed for ever under the burden of fate. Why ? Listen to these verses of *Remembrance :*

> I have seen other things than the leaves from the bowers,
> Or the froth of the waves, fall as idly as words;
> Fairer things have I seen than the perfume of flowers
>   And the song of the birds;
>
> Sadder things on this earth have my moist eyes deplored
> Than the dead Juliet in her bridals of white;
> Darker things than the toast that her lover outpoured
>   To the angel of night;

What was this horrible, funereal thing that the unhappy poet saw ? He tells us:

> I have seen my one love—love her ever I must—
> As a whitened sepulchre, from which light had fled,
> The dark living grave, all shrouded in dust,
>   Of our love that was dead;
>
> Our poor love, the sweet child we had nightly enfurled
> In the warmth of our hearts when the moon o'er us shone;
> *Alas ! more than a life to my life; 'twas a world*
>   *That had died and was gone.*

A world ! Neither more nor less !

Yes, all these glorious and immortal figures of speech that are used for the extolling of sorrow, these " reeds that the wind bears away from our hands," these " baptisms in unhappiness," these " dews of tears " that a man needs to be healed, these " declamations like blood-dripping swords," these " chants of despair " and " broken lyres " and " immortal sobs," the whole of Musset, in a word, in his sincere laments, have one single cause—the departure of a faithless love ! Surely this is a child crying because his doll has fallen into the sea ?

IV

Is this a poet of sorrow ? What ! For thousands and thousands of years poor humanity has dragged itself over the earth in pursuit of a happiness that ever recedes before it like a mirage; for long ages men, races, and empires have clashed, urged on by a destiny of which none of us yet knows the secret; from the dawn of time we have held up to heaven hands that implore unceasingly and begin ever anew; during the whole of time we have struggled and stumbled through the bloody darkness—and you would call the man who, in the midst of all this tragedy, has suffered a little from a woman's caprice the poet of sorrow ! No, no. By all the disinherited of fate who are born, are reared, and die in wretched dens, by all the vanquished of life, all the martyrs, all the apostles, all the dead heroes, all who were wounded by the monster, all who were crucified for the ideal—no, to be thwarted in love is not a great sorrow.

In fact—let us have the courage to say it—no personal grievance, no domestic unhappiness, however painful the wound, however holy the cause, even if it were the most heartrending of separations, a mother's loss of her son or a son's loss of his mother, suffices to justify a work of eternal tears or to make us the interpreters of an immense tragedy.

For our mourning to be sublime there must be something greater than the inevitable troubles that await all of us, repeated millions of times a day over the surface of the globe, falling indifferently upon the wicked and the good, the rich and the poor, the young and the old. Really noble and heroic hearts must and can conceal their intimate sorrows. If our sobs are to be justified, the cause must be beyond and above ourselves. The only great joys and sorrows are public joys and sorrows.

Those who have known great sorrow are the men who have seen in flames the cities in which the dreams of their ancestors had taken shape: the men who have seen their whole race, with all their glory, their hope, and their gods, reduced to slavery; the men who witnessed the fall of civilisations they had thought eternal; the men who saw empires and worlds brought to naught.

It is a great sorrow when Prometheus makes the mountain ring with his anger at the evils which torment his beloved humanity; when Priam and Achilles, in face of mourning Troy, weep together over the long line of corpses on the shore and over all the misfortunes that threaten both peoples; when Æneas tells Dido of the sack of Troy and the destruction of his race; when the exiled Dante, forgetting his personal misfortunes, thinks only of Italy torn by civil hatreds and calls it *di dolore ostello ;* when the Hebrew poets, by the river in a strange land, hang their harps on the willows and lament the loss of Jerusalem; when on Golgotha, lit by lightning, Christ utters his supreme cry to the humanity that will suffer for ever. But to speak about a great sorrow, to weep out one's soul in desperate sobs, to conjure up the most tragic figures, to call to witness all the forces of nature and all the ages of human history, to declare oneself a victim of the gods just because Dame Sand has gone off with the solid Pagello, really—I must say it, though I be disgraced for ever in the eyes of all girls in the first flush of puberty and all young men of erotic dreams—it is a mockery of human misery, a sacrilege of sorrow.

V

That is why in this book we cannot separate Musset from George Sand. It is no blind chance that brought them together in a common life and keeps their names together in a romantic legend. They had to meet each other, to love and hate each other, by an inevitable predestination.

While George Sand, the woman, extols passion in every note of her victorious eloquence, proclaims it queen, and hurls it " as a blind force against all the obstacles of civilisation," Alfred de Musset, the man, humbly and publicly recognises the other's victory, resigns himself to all the torture and despair of defeat, and in the end even finds an unspeakable charm in the weakness of his overthrow. The distinguished and fatal pair go far beyond, not merely the contents of an adventurous story, but beyond the judgment of the critic of books. For all time they symbolise in the history of letters all the disorders of sentimental frenzy, all the immeasurable vanity of love.

CHARLES BAUDELAIRE

The only true reality is in dreams.—Ch. B.: *Artificial Paradises*.

CHAPTER VII

CHARLES BAUDELAIRE

I

I HAVE always loved Baudelaire.* Even now, when I propose to dissect his work and analyse the unwholesome perfumes which rise from his " sickly flowers," I find, for the hundredth or the thousandth time, an unutterable pleasure in plunging into the warm, enfolding atmosphere of his genius. There have been, and will again be, perhaps, certainly more bracing and more uplifting poets; but there was never one who was more captivating, more sincere, and more profound. If you read him once, you can never forget him. His verses grip a man's memory as if with iron claws which cauterise and tear, and leave red scars for ever. In the energy, the conciseness, and the sober splendour of his style he is the most classical of all the poets of the nineteenth century. In boldness of metaphor, the startling character of his figures, the boldness of his ellipses, and the sprightliness of his lyrics, he is the greatest innovator amongst the romanticists. From the literary point of view he is complete; and in a century in which poets were loose in regard to inspiration and sentiment he, like Théophile Gautier, set the example of severe, unified, synthetic work. And what charm in his words ! What a miraculous gift of conjuring up worlds by the sound of syllables and rhymes ! What magic of music and colour !

* See Note 6 (at end of volume).

Degeneration in the Great French Masters

Is there in the whole of French literature a more dazzling vision than that suggested by the fine verses of *La Chevelure*?

> A loudly echoing harbour, where my soul may hold
> To quaff, the silver cup of colours, scents, and sounds,
> Wherein the vessels glide upon a sea of gold,
> And stretch their mighty arms, the glory to enfold
> Of virgin skies, where never-ending heat abounds.*

Is there anywhere a more robust and more perfect verse than this quatrain of the *Vin des chiffoniers*?

> He hears the oaths of mortals, laws dictates,
> The wicked smites, the sufferer vindicates;
> And, 'neath a sky like purple dais hung,
> Hears the full glory of his virtues sung.

Is there a more sublime flight than that which closes the poem *Les Phares*?

> It is the mightiest witness that could rise
> To prove our dignity, O Lord, to Thee;
> This sob that rolls from age to age, and dies
> Upon the verge of Thy Eternity.†

Yes, it is easy to understand how he is loved, how he has influence, for none had a fuller measure of the wizard's power. Moreover, while he is charming as a poet, as a man, in spite of his defects, he wins from us by the sincerity of his sorrow and the proud disinterestedness of his life an irresistible, indestructible sympathy. It is impossible not to feel pity for the sufferings of the man who wrote *Bénédiction*, *L'Irréparable*, *Chant d'Automne*, *Le Mauvais Moine*, *Un Voyage à Cythère*, and so many other poems; particularly that admirable and sublime *Voyage*, the dome and synthesis of his work, one of the most moving poems in any literature.

* Cyril Scott's translation, Baudelaire's *Flowers of Evil*.
† Translation by F. P. Sturm, *Poems of C. Baudelaire*.

He remains, with Flaubert, a severe lesson in literary conscientiousness, and his example teaches us that the first duty of a true poet is to devote his whole life and work to the glorification of the language he has inherited; and that to sustain and augment the prestige of that language is the best means of showing oneself piously loyal to the race from which one has sprung.

Yet the magician in the art of style and the science of the heart, this great writer, is, in spite of all, a " bad master." Possibly no other has had a more disturbing, more saddening, more discouraging influence on the generations that followed him.

He himself, indeed, with his severe conscience and eminent sincerity, was the first to acknowledge this. Even before his work appeared, he indicated the profound viciousness of it by entitling it *Flowers of Evil.* Since his death, even during life, he gave rise to fierce controversies, not only in literature, but also in the courts; and I will not seek, after so many others and himself, to discover the evil influence of his genius. But it seems to me that both they and he are wrong in assigning the causes of his moral ailment. He has been hated and loved passionately, like all who show the tyranny of a powerful personality in everything they do. But enemies and friends have been unjust or blind in their reciprocal violence. While the one class boldly accused him of immorality, and even denied that he had genius, the others raised him upon a pedestal that was not of the earth, and enthroned him as an infernal divinity. He himself, by a tendency that is very natural in the human mind, disposing him to enlarge his defects rather than correct them, was inclined to fancy himself invested with some vague mission of darkness; and over his incurable evil he cast a sort of satanic purple, streaked with fire.

141

So far did he go that no one—in my belief, at least—ever saw the real reason for his evil work: a very simple, very human, unfortunately very common reason—so common that it took all his genius to lift it to the height of poetic beauty.

II

No, Baudelaire was not immoral, as his short-sighted critics said; but he was demoralising, which is quite a different thing. He was a dissipator of energy. In his own person first, then in others, he broke the mainspring of action and strength.

His evil was, *the fear of action*. This he hides from himself under the pleasant title, *the love of dreaming*. But they are merely two different expressions for the same weakness, and that is *cowardice in face of life*.

All of us have, more or less, a disposition to cast aside the burden of daily exigencies; to lie down by the roadside, to close our eyes, to take our flight, under the soothing murmur of the wind and the caresses of the sun, to the unbounded kingdom of dreams. We all believe, more or less, at one time or another, that we are unjustly placed in the human drove, and it seems to us that we have a right to escape, to live as we will, or refuse to live by the rule; to fly away, in dreams or in solitude, no matter where, so that it be somewhere outside the world. And we deck this vice of our nature in the most florid phrases. We persuade ourselves that it is an elegance of soul, a superiority of mind.

Ah, the dream! The invisible seducer, the most subtle of the demons that hover about us, the most seductive and most deceptive form, mirage, or cloud, the worst of errors and weaknesses. What evil it does to the man it seduces! How many human lives there are of which it

has stolen one half! How many that it has entirely
absorbed! How sad is the ultimate fall to which it leads
us! What insipidity we have after its perfumes, what
gnashing of teeth after its murmurs, what ashes from
its torch! Slayer of heroes, devourer of genius, who
can count the number of its victims? Sometimes it
dances about us in the shimmer of voluptuous robes;
sometimes it makes splendid festivals of our future glory;
sometimes it takes the deceitful form of action itself,
and intoxicates us with the great deeds we are going to
accomplish later. But whether it is sweet, magnificent,
or heroic, it is always the enemy of the present, always
appealing to the future. It constantly dangles marvellous
futures before our eyes, and, whenever we are disgusted
with the present, it whispers: " To-morrow, to-morrow."
We make ourselves drunk with this to-morrow that
never comes; and the more the dream possesses us, the
more we wish it to possess us further. A day comes
when we awaken, old and tottering, reduced to naught
in the present, hopeless as to the future, hating mankind,
hating and despising ourselves, mourning the time lost,
bowed down with remorse and anguish; and as dreaming
is then as indispensable to us as bad alcohol is to the
drunkard, we seek it in drink, in debauch, in the darkest
excitements — in " artificial paradises "—until the day
when, finding it no longer, we summon death to set us
free.

That is the fatal decline of dreaming, the development of this abdication of life, this reluctance for action.
That is, on analysis, traced to its cause and worked out
in its consequences, the work of Baudelaire. That is
why it is, in truth, the supreme " flower of evil."

III

The coward's dream—that is what Baudelaire enjoyed, what he expressed in all its forms. His despair, his misanthropy, his revolts, his troubles, his terrors, his love of non-existence, are only so many developments of this initial weakness—the fear of life. With all his gifts as a humanist and all his marvellous gifts as a poet he had also, to the degree of genius, the state of soul of the vagabond who wanders off to sleep in the fields, shunning the lodging and the workshop, and at night soaks in the public-house. He refused manly action. All the rest is the penalty for this.

We may take the whole of his work, the *Flowers of Evil* as well as the *Poems in Prose*, and we shall see that, line by line, word by word, we may reduce everything to these sentiments:

1. Fear and disgust of life, boredom, dislike and contempt of men.
2. Refuge in the dream, in travel, and in the night.
3. Refuge in pleasure, debauch, and artificial paradises.
4. Regret for the loss of healthy life, action, and time.
5. Remorse and anguish.
6. Refuge in death, desire for non-existence, appeal to an unknown life.

And all these succeed each other as logically as the successive leaps of a waterfall in a gorge.

We should have to quote half his works to show how often he exhibits fear of life, and of time, which is its sensuous form. Listen to this strident cry of one of his prose-poems:

Yes, time has appeared once more. Time is now ruler; and with the hideous old man comes all his demoniac train of Remembrances, Regrets, Spasms, Fears, Anguishes, Nightmares, Angers, and Nervous Fits.

144

Charles Baudelaire

I assure you that the seconds are now strongly and solemnly accented, and each of them says, as it leaps from the pendulum: *I am life, insupportable, implacable life.*

It would be impossible to express this fear in clearer terms. Here, however, are verses which complete the prose-poetry:

> Why, I envy the lot of the vile soulless beasts
> That can bury themselves in the stupor of sleep,
> So slow does the progress of time seem to creep.

And these:

> A gaunt graveyard am I, by the pale moon abhorred.
>
>   *   *   *   *   *
>
> An old boudoir am I, full of roses that fade.
>
>   *   *   *   *   *
>
> An old sphinx that the world in its lightness ignores,
> That, unheeded by men in the flush of their days,
> Chants its sombre refrain to the setting sun's rays.

And as hatred of men is an outcome of this *tædium vitæ*, the fundamental vice of dreamers, we meet it at every turn, and it assumes the deceptive appearance of a jealous and wounded superiority.

> All those that he would cherish shrink from him with fear,
> And some that, waxen bold by his tranquillity,
> Endeavour hard some grievance from his heart to tear,
> And make on him the trial of their ferocity.
>
> CYRIL SCOTT.

Of this contempt of men was born the famous symbol of the *Albatross* :

> Not unlike is the poet to the prince of the clouds,
> Who disports in the storm and for shafts is too fleet;
> *From companionship banned, 'midst the jeers of the crowds,*
> He has wings of a giant and disdains mortal feet.

That is the dominant note of his work: a horror of normal life, and, consequently, a *love of dreaming*, of

everything that distracts him from life, of travel, of the
night, of the clouds, and all that is vague and formless:

> What dost thou love, then, marvellous stranger ?
> I love the clouds . . . the clouds which pass away yonder . .
> the marvellous clouds.

Read his *Mauvais Vitrier,* his *Crépuscule du soir,* and
especially his *Invitation au voyage,* in which he sighs:

> Dreams ! Dreams ever ! The more ambitious and delicate the
> soul is, the farther it goes from the possible in dreams.

How many fine verses he has in which we have all
drunk the philtre of dreams:

> To some land will I go where all things lie at rest
> In a languorous swoon, that from year to year lasts.
> Tresses strong, be the wave to bear me on thy crest !
> Ebon sea, in thy depths is a dream of the blest,
> Of rowers and sails, pennants gay and tall masts !

The love of travelling which Baudelaire, like all slaves
of the dream, had in a passionate degree, is merely one
way of fleeing from life. Travel is a dream materialising
in constantly renewed forms.

In the *Poems in Prose* there is a page that expresses
with penetrating emotion the sentiment felt by all who
have known the joy of being cradled in the voluptuousness
of the waves during a long voyage, so that one's heart
tastes the delight of an infinite dream:

> Like some priest from whom his divinity has been stolen, I
> could not, without heart-rending bitterness, tear myself away
> from this monstrously seductive sea. . . .
> In saying farewell to this incomparable beauty I was stricken
> to death; and that is why, when my companions cried " At last !"
> I could only exclaim "Already !"

The whole fear of life weeps in that simple " Already ";
the whole love of dreams breathes in it.

> Take me far, sluggard train ! Haste thee, ship, far away !
> For the mud where we stand is compacted of tears.

Night also is one of the great gates of the dream. How the poet loves it ! How plainly one sees that his favourite star is not the sun, the inspirer of action, but the moon, that " luminous poison," which whispers to the woman who has fallen under its influence:

Thou shalt be the queen of men with green eyes, whose throat also I have closed in my nightly caresses; of those who love the sea, the boundless sea, tumultuous and green, the formless and multiform water, the place where they are not, the woman they know not, the perfumes which unman the will, and the wild voluptuous animals which are the symbols of their follies !

But the dream, travel, and night, soothing as they are, have, unfortunately, an end:

> And opening wide my flame-lit eyes,
> I saw the horror of my den,
> And felt, as I essayed to rise,
> Accursed care pierce me again.
>
> With funeral note the sullen bell
> Announced inexorably 'twas noon;
> Yet all the world was dark as hell—
> A world I saw again too soon.

Do you follow the fatal progress of the evil ? Since, after all, we cannot escape " the horror of the den " and " the darkness"—the darkness of noon, notice, which is so miserable in comparison with a dream—we will try stimulants to bring back the vanished dreams. So the dreamer goes on to pleasure, drink, debauch, and artificial paradises.

Sorry paradises they are. Listen:

One must be drunk always. Everything is in that; it is the only question. If you would not feel the horrible burden of Time that breaks your shoulders, and bows you to the earth, you must intoxicate yourself unceasingly.

But with what ? With wine, with poetry, or with virtue—as you please. But intoxicate yourself.

It is easy to understand how Baudelaire came to sing the poetry of wine so marvellously:

> Not for that, bottle deep, would a wise man reject
> The sweet-smelling balm which thy paunch doth inject
> In the heart of the poet athirst for thy wine.
>
> Hope and youth, and the fulness of life are thy gifts;
> —Also pride, the strong spirit that drooping souls lifts
> To the raptures of triumph, to levels divine.

As to pleasure and debauch, listen how they become a sinister refuge for the lover of dreams:

> And gently balanced on the wing
> Of the wild whirlwind we will ride,
> Rejoicing with the joyous thing.
>
> My sister, floating side by side,
> Fly we unceasing whither gleams
> The distant heaven of my dreams.
>
> F. P. STURM.

And how far we are from the harmless tol-de-rols of the tavern in this terrible cry:

> When wilt thou bury me, impure-armed Debauch?

Is there anything idyllic and tender in this recourse to the sorrowful Cytheræa:

> In thy isle, goddess, naught but a gibbet remained,
> And its chain tossed a figure of myself in the wind.
> —Lord God! of Thy mercy, brace Thou my mind,
> To look on my heart and my limbs unashamed.

Shame is the fatal end of this tragic pilgrimage; then the man possessed by the dream is reduced to taking refuge in *artificial paradises*. Baudelaire has written a whole work on opium and hashish, the dangerous consolers of the desperate.

It is, unfortunately, all in vain; it is a mockery of a duel with life, inexorable to those who rebel against it. And so the poet, ferreted out of all his precarious retreats, feels all the vanity of his dreams and all the cowardice of his evasion, and he weeps over the time he has lost, the activity he neglected, the life in the sun which he refused. Toward the close of his life Villon cried:

> Ah! had I at my task remained,
> In those young days, so swiftly flown,
> And from the ways of vice refrained,
> A house I'd have, and bed of down.

So Baudelaire murmurs his sorrowful regret, but he gives nobler motives than the " house " and the " bed of down." He says to himself:

> Anon strikes the hour of the Almighty's fate,
> When the voice of fair virtue, thy virginal bride,
> When repentance itself, the last refuge of pride,
> Will say, *Die, aged coward, 'tis too late.*

On the other hand, he addresses his sickly Muse:

> I wish, as the health-giving fragrance I cull,
> That thy breast with strong thoughts could for ever be full,
> And that, rhythmic'ly flowing, thy Christian blood
>
> Could resemble the old-time metrical flood,
> Where each in his turn reigned the father of Rhymes,
> Phœbus, and Pan, lord of harvest times.
>
> Scott.

But age has come, and the heart is no longer strong enough to receive the solar radiation. Inexorable time has had its revenge, and the poet humbly confesses it:

> Now the autumn chill conquers the fire of my blood,
> Now the time has arrived for the spade and the rake,
> To restore the smooth earth where the water in flood
> Has left holes like great graves in its terrible wake. . . .
>
> Oh, unutterable sadness!   Time eateth our life,
> And the dark hostile power that gnaweth our heart
> Waxes fat on our blood, and grows strong for the strife.

What a sorrow to feel that one has not accomplished one's mission, that one has refused to live!   The poet's anger rises. He pours invectives upon God, whom he holds responsible. He believes that the world has betrayed him in not giving him the elements of an heroic life:

> As for me, I go satisfied out of a world
> Wherein action has proved not the sister of dream.

The unhappy man! It is he himself who would have nothing to do with action. However, he knows this well, and, in spite of the clenched fists he raises to heaven, the dolorous pilgrim of the Dream falls speedily back upon the lucid vision in his soul. Then comes the odious remorse, the last voluptuousness of cowards, the bloody and rending intoxication of the evil experienced or done.

The lines in which Baudelaire has expressed all the anguish of remorse are so famous and so numerous that I need do no more than refer to them:

> Hast thou ever, good angel, the deep anguish known
> Of black shame and remorse, of sobs and fatigue?
> * * * * *
> Can we stifle the voice of this aged remorse?
> * * * * *
> Let us blow out the lamp, my friend;
> In the dark let us hide ourselves.

And at length this sublime figure, which has become classical:

> By some mystery of vengeance, whose work is divine,
> From the brute sunk in sleep, see, an angel awakes.

But the dreadful cycle of the Dream has now come to the stage of paroxysms of torment, and, finding himself tired of dreaming, incapable of taking up life once more, riven with remorse, the unhappy man, who has gone through the whole of hell on earth, has only one resource left—to call upon death, sometimes hailing it as annihilation, sometimes dreaming of finding a new life in it:

Charles Baudelaire

> Black companions, ye worms, without ears and without eyes,
> See, there comes a new corpse in freedom and joy !

Need we quote *Le Goût du néant ?* The title is enough :

> And grim Time swallows me as the minutes go by . . .
> Avalanche, would'st thou sweep me away in thy rush ?

Listen, also, to the famous sonnets which he gathered together under the general title, *Death :*

> It is death that consoles, yet restores us to life !
>
> *   *   *   *   *
>
> 'Tis the portal that opens new heavens to us !
>
> *   *   *   *   *
>
> Like new sun in the heavens, death soars above all,
> And its kiss reawakens the flowers of our soul.

Who needs to be reminded of *The Death of Lovers ?* the poem so full of suggestions of pain, which the nerve-tainted constantly murmur :

> We'll have beds that exhale the sweet odours of earth.

We all know it by heart. Every Bohemian has set it to music. But what need is there for us to wander through the whole of Baudelaire's works ? One single poem is enough. It contains all the others. It is synthetic ; as formidable as some mirror in which the rays of a black sun are focussed. It is called *The Voyage,* and is a masterpiece of beauty. Read that attentively, for it closes and sums up the *Flowers of Evil.* Passing from verse to verse, you go through all the mazes of impotence and dizziness of brain, until you reach the sonorous and magnificent appeal at the end :

> O death, old Captain, it is time, put forth !
> We have grown weary of the gloomy north.
>
> F. P. STURM.

IV

Have we now gone far enough down the winding stair that leads from the Dream to Death ? Have we followed far enough the descent of the poor poet's soul ? Do we see whither the fear of action takes a man ?

Baudelaire's friends, his admirers and pupils, have been so much seduced by his enthralling genius that they have tried to see in him the supreme expression of a civilisation. They make him an apostle of pessimism and a prophet of decadence. That is going very far and very high to find the explanation of a very common evil: an evil, unfortunately, of all ages and all lands, with plenty of examples round about us. Possibly these examples are more numerous and more apparent in times of social crisis, when the wretched state of the public health suffers all sorts of individual infirmities to display themselves; but it is a universal evil, and its root is in our very nature. That is, in fact, why the picture of it is so dangerous when the gift of poetry, with its manifold seductions, adds its charm to the natural temptations which each of us has in his own being. Can you tell me any way in which we can defend ourselves against the magic of Baudelaire's poems ? Endowed, as he was, to produce the finest verse, such a poet could, if he had so willed, have borne us into the world of heroes. What can he not do, then, when he drags us with him to the facile instincts of the Dream and Inaction ? He finds too many echoes in the obscure depths of our being for us to fail to respond to him; his voice, moreover, is irresistible. Immense, therefore, is the evil for which he is responsible ! Baudelaire was, like Musset, a propagator of moral cowardice. It is to those two that whole generations owe it that they were not able to live, or that they lingered too long in the non-existence of revery.

The inventor of epics, the dramatist, the novelist act upon us by means of their heroes, but the lyric poet has a direct influence on our souls; it is his own personality that he projects upon ours.   He is himself the hero of his poems, and, if he is a genius, we need to make an effort, which is at first impossible, to resist his suggestions. When he is bracing and sunny, like a Hugo or a Lamartine, he imparts to us a little of his strength in the robust clearness of his words.   But when he is sickly and disturbed, when he takes pleasure in the emanations from dark things instead of straining toward the light, the disasters which he causes in the hearts of the young are as terrible as a poisoned caress.

In spite of their difference in temperament and genius, Musset and Baudelaire did the same unhealthy work, for both, unfortunately, were tainted with the same inability to act.   Both sought refuge in dreaming and all the horrors which follow upon it.   The first, more accessible and of common stuff, acted like a slow poison upon the wavering souls of sentimental young men; the second, greater, nobler, and prouder, drew choice spirits to himself, and he held out to every wounded pride and torn illusion the quick but dangerous remedy of the maddening opium of his lyrics.   And from both one learned easily that there was a high distinction in shunning life.

That is why, while we may love these harmonious and seductive poets, we cannot too carefully guard ourselves against the disturbing influence of their genius.   Yet, let us avoid these morbid effects of night and isolation; let us flee the viscous temptations of idleness and fear; let us not listen to the cajoling whispers with which death consoles cowards. Life, sonorous and luminous, with all its rays, its turmoil, and its battles, rises and rises again unceasingly; and it flings out as far as the horizon an appeal which none has the right to neglect. Man was made for action as surely as water for the waving of the sea and seed to ferment in the bowels of the earth. Woe to the man who would evade his destiny! In his terror he will suffer all the madness of the evils which courage would have crushed. Woe to the man who hides in dreams when he is called to live!

> No matter where! No matter where! If 'tis outside the world,

cries the poet. And we must answer:

> No matter where! No matter where! If it be in mankind.

Flowers of Evil, terrible mandragoras, magical and funereal flowers that spring up in the malediction of the dark, who will come with breath strong enough to blow away for ever the perfume of your poisoned corollas? Who will bring out toward new mornings the lovely and sane flowers of light, the victorious lilies and triumphant roses, whose happy colours will, on the festivals of the soul, be the bright flags of works of strength and joy that are yet to come?

GUSTAVE FLAUBERT

Existence is tolerable only in the delirium of letters. But the delirium has its lucid intervals, and it is then that one is bored.—
G. F., in letter to Ernest Peydeau.

CHAPTER VIII

GUSTAVE FLAUBERT

I NEVER think of Gustave Flaubert without recalling, in broad outline, the heroic, truculent, and fruitless adventure of the Norman warriors who, from the ninth to the eleventh century, threatened to conquer the whole world, yet two centuries later disappeared altogether from history.

I

The spread of the Norman race across a stupefied Europe is an *Iliad* or an *Odyssey*. But what a barbarous epic, at once savage and splendid, it was while it lasted !

See them cruising in their boats along the shores of the Carolingian Empire. They reach the Mediterranean, and such is the terror they inspire that Charlemagne himself weeps with distress at Narbonne. As soon as the great Emperor has gone, the invasion begins. They pour in by all the rivers at once. As they pass, they plunder Rouen, Nantes, Tours, Angers, Saintes, and Bordeaux. They burn Trèves, Cologne, and Aix-la-Chapelle. Now they have penetrated to the very heart of Gaul; and Paris, twice sacked, is twice on the point of becoming their capital. Are these barbaric wanderers of the coast about to master and govern the glorious West ? Men fear it for a moment; and the old Roman world recedes everywhere in terror before this mysterious people, which seems to pour out in waves from every sea.

But it does not happen. They are still too young to

become masters of the world. They satisfy their turbu-
lent ambition with booty and ransoms. From the cities
they have invaded they retire as quickly as they had
come; and when a corner of this immense feudal Europe
is granted them by treaty, they cast themselves upon it
like children upon a new toy, happy to establish themselves in their turn in the unexpected character of lords
of the soil.

But the migratory and conquering genius of the race
slumbers only a single century on the fat lands of Neustria.
Hardly have they obtained, in three or four generations,
a sufficient contact with the Gallo-Roman civilisation,
when these Normans are off for fresh adventures. For
a moment they dispute the rising empire of France with
the Capetians. But Paris is too near to them; they need
the attraction of some distant unknown. They rise from
their newly established feoffs, and, partly by sea and
partly by land, carry out at one and the same time two
of the gigantic events of the Middle Ages—the conquest
of England and the conquest of Italy.

Tancred de Hauteville, Robert Guiscard, Roger of
Sicily, William the Bastard—what Achilles, what Aga-
memnons, what Ulysses even; for their cunning and
subtlety are not inferior to their savage bravery, and the
most romantic of these barbaric heroes, the ravager of
Rome and Apulia, bore the name of " Guiscard," which
means " the Wary." They are no longer roaming pirates,
hated of all peoples. They are now the friends and sup-
porters of Popes. Even the Greeks appeal for their
aid. They do not wait now until a corner of a province
is given to them; they rapidly found vast kingdoms and
dream of empires. Are they at last about to carry out
the definitive conquest of Europe ? Are they, robust
and fiery race as they are, about to take up the destiny

of ancient Rome, and, as masters of the sea from London to Constantinople, to renew the decrepit East ?

No, it is a whirlwind that passes as it came: a storm on the land, a cyclone on the sea. It is only a dream. Hardly have they entered an ancient country as conquerors, and settled down in their castles and feudal domains, than they are lost in the midst of the surrounding populations, as the eddies of any angry torrent are lost in the slow, calm waves of the river which it joins.

So little remained in France of the early conquerors that in the thirteenth century Normandy was the most loyal province of the Crown. By 1200 the Norman race was completely absorbed and annihilated under the skies of Sicily and Calabria; and in England the last descendants of the famous adventurers, apart from a few barons, were about to exterminate each other in the Wars of the Roses. Wherever they entered as conquerors, the vanquished race slowly, in the course of time, resumed its natural development, its name, its tongue, and its interrupted destiny. Not an idiom, not a single institution, not a single law, is left that belongs properly to the Normans. They are the nomads of history; yet they die of their stability.

Strange and deceptive fortune ! Why is this race stricken with such sterility that, though it conquers everywhere, it founds nothing anywhere ? It is because the Normans had all the external splendour of adventurers and warriors, but none of the deeper virtues which make men civilisers and creators of empires. They had no aim. They did not know what they wanted. They wanted nothing except to fight and loot. They had not the least idea of duration, not the dimmest ideal of the future. For them *existence was tolerable only in delirium ;* and, as the most intoxicating delirium is that of battles and looting, they took every occasion to satisfy their robust temperament with its frenzied joys. There was in them, indeed, a sort of destructive and negative fatalism, and this made them hostile to everything that policed races call " civilisation." Even when they were lords and princes of flourishing kingdoms, they had a brutal contempt of, a furious anger against, the rest of the race. Consider them at Rome, whither Robert Guiscard had led them. They did more harm in a few days to the Eternal City than the barbarians of the Danube and the Vistula had done in six centuries. In England their cruelty to the conquered race was the act of exasperated savages. They were tainted with heroic misanthropy. They were the knights of non-existence.

Nevertheless, in spite of the emptiness and storminess of their historical career, they left here and there traces of their passage in works of great external splendour. They were childish and violent, but magnificent, barbarians. They loved pomp and ostentation. Of the whole civilisation they found in the West the one thing that charmed them was the splendour of everything that served for the visible ornamentation of life. They loved purple and gold, heavy feasts of prodigal luxury, bright colours, opulent and complicated architecture. They were as delighted as children to finger rich fabrics. Roger, first King of Naples and Amalfi, wore over his tunic a scarlet stole, all embroidered and fringed with gold, sparkling with jewels. William, after the conquest of England, went to Rouen, and there for several days he held royal festival for all the knights of France and Aquitania, and spread before their eyes all the precious vessels, the horn cups, the treasures and marvels he had looted from the vanquished race.

The famous tapestry of Bayeux shows how far they

pushed their love of plastic beauty. Then there are their superb churches and abbeys. These conquerors, who founded no city and no law anywhere, leave on every hand buildings upon which they have lavished the whole wealth of contemporary art. Neither innovators nor inventors, they borrow from the peoples they conquer all the forms which please the eye. They are Gothic in the north, Byzantine and Arab in Sicily and Salerno. But their passion, though fierce and tasteless, is sincere. They are like young and impatient heirs who, obtaining possession of an old and rich estate, leave the fields fallow to build towers and mansions, and adorn their walls with gold and silk. The fields are occupied by others, and the heirs die or are dispossessed; but the splendour remains, a witness to the passing of these light-minded and opulent children.

That is why, whenever one now recalls, in the light of history, the prodigious and foolish epic of the Normans, one sees in the distance a few isolated monuments, of sumptuous and unequal beauty, against a red and disordered background of vanity and destruction.

II

The whole soul of the Norman heroes is, by a process of atavistic transmission, found in the soul and the work of Gustave Flaubert.

I know, of course, that one must not press ethnological theories too far in the study of a literary man. It would be pedantic and foolish to attempt to impose upon a poetic genius the theory—a theory that is sometimes narrow and often hazardous—of heredity and environment. It frequently happens that genius is an exception. And can we accurately estimate all the mingled influences at work in the slow formation of a great man ? I would add even that, in my opinion, it rarely happens that a powerful writer is the clear pro-jection of an ancient race, to such an extent that you cannot study one without recalling the other. I know only two in contemporary literature in whose case the atavism is plain and indisputable. One of them, born at Maillane, in the ancient Hellenic colony of Glanum, is Mistral, in whom was concentrated the whole soul of Greece. The other is Flaubert, a direct descendant of the companions of Robert Guiscard, who passes, after eight centuries, from the passion of war to the passion of letters, and brings to it the same magnificence and the same vanity.

It requires no effort to discover this superb Norman heredity in Flaubert. He himself claimed it, with truculent pride. He loved to call attention to the fact that he had the blue eyes, the light complexion, the heavy and drooping moustache, the full body, and the keen appetite of the great adventurers who conquered Sicily. All who knew him agree in describing him as a paladin at sea in our bourgeois age. From his remote ancestors he had temper and impatience, a need of constant agita-tion and movement, a chronic state of excitement, and a certain chivalry urging him always to set out for battles and massacres. He could not mention an enemy with-out consigning him to the most execrable torments. When one reads his letters, one feels that, if he had lived eight centuries earlier, such as he was born, he would, like the others, have killed the horses of the Greek mes-sengers with his fists, or eviscerated citizens of Rome, at the slightest contradiction.

I linger thus, deliberately, over the epic of the Normans, not in order to crush the great Flaubert under the burden of his race of sterile destiny, but in order to make clear, in the light of the past, why his magnificent work is, nevertheless, so desolating and so futile.

For it is time that we came to the proper subject of this essay: time to say that the author of *Madame Bovary, Salammbô, Bouvard et Pécuchet, La Tentation*, and *L'Éducation sentimentale*, was one of the "bad masters" of the last century, and one whose influence was the more disturbing as his mastership is beyond question.

How could we explain a man so admirable in his life, of so noble a heart, of a mind so impassioned for beauty, producing an unhealthy work, if we did not find in his nature some fatalism of which he was himself the first and the worst victim? It is impossible not to love Flaubert. Was any man braver, prouder, more generous, more worthy of affection? How fine and disinterested was his passion for letters! What single-minded devotion to his friends! What proofs of nobility even in his hatreds! And his work—what a titanic strain after greatness!

Yet the work is empty and desolating. How can we understand it? I have sought the reason in ethnic predestination: the only reason that really explains the anomaly. I could not lay all the blame on Flaubert alone. "He seemed to bear all the fatigue of a futile attempt to scale some heaven," said the brothers Goncourt. No; he bore within him the fatalism of a race that had slept for eight centuries, and had suddenly, after a silent elaboration, reawakened in the brain of a genius. He was a synthesis of the vices and the virtues of his ancestors:

Delicta majorum immeritus lues.

We shall see that his weaknesses and his greatness are a faithful mirror of the greatness and the weaknesses of the epic of the Normans.

III

What, in fact, is the fundamental vice of Flaubert's work, the vice which has from the start made it harmful to every mind that was impregnated with it? It is an incurable and absolute nihilism, the denial of all patient striving toward a higher ideal; it is, in a word, a violent hatred of civilisation. You will find this hatred break out in angry terms in the whole of Flaubert's correspondence; and it is always present, open or latent, in his novels, sometimes ironic, sometimes sullenly angry, sometimes resigned and grieved at its own powerlessness. It is, indeed, the one invariable background of a scattered work that has no other unity. One feels at every turn that Gustave Flaubert detests men, and is angry because they are not all as he is. It is a frank, truculent, even heroic misanthropy, like that of his ancestors. It is capable of deeds of chivalry, and it is just as capable of deceiving by its bluster. But it is misanthropic all the same. Less wicked and treacherous than the work of Stendhal, it has, nevertheless, the same issue—a horror of all organised society. Flaubert's work is essentially anti-social; that is its defect. "We are all in a desert," he said; "no one understands anybody." In his view one man was necessarily the enemy of another, and all society was a game of dupes, fools, and scoundrels. He disdained its mechanism, despised its laws, and enjoyed only the external movement in its more picturesque features. So felt the companions of Hauteville when they marched across Italy. As, however, Flaubert cannot have the satisfaction of looting Rome and sacking Apulia, he must assail this society, which he regards as stupid, by sarcasm, irony, and a fury of eloquence. All the efforts of the human sufferers do but provoke a

burst of thunderous laughter from this handsome bar-
barian. All the dreams of a better race he massacres
pitilessly; either in the symbols of the *Tentation* or of
Salammbô, or by personifying them in characters which
he deliberately makes ridiculous, as he conceives men,
such as Frédéric Moreau, Bouvard and Pécuchet, the
Abbé Bournisien, and poor Homais.

It is said that shortly before his death, Émile Zola
said to his friends that, if he had time, he would some
day take up the defence of Homais against Flaubert's
irony. I do not know whether the author of the Rougon-
Macquart series would have had serenity enough to do
this, for it would require a complete freedom from combative passion. But it was a fine piece of audacity to
think of it, for one runs the risk of incurring ridicule
when one sets out to defend a man who is regarded as
ridiculous. Moreover, Zola would only have defended
Homais on a side which is open to controversy. Like
nearly all the writers of the last century, Zola had strong
passions and prejudices. The impartiality which I try—
so very imperfectly—to attain, as is necessary when one
would understand all the weaknesses of man, I invoke
here when I venture to say that Homais is a piece of
injustice perpetrated by Flaubert; as Tartufe is on the
part of Molière, and Don Quixote on the part of Cervantes.
In the person of Don Quixote, indeed, it is genuine chivalry
which the prisoner of Lepanto ridicules; in the person of
Tartufe, Molière attacks the true believer; in the person
of Homais, Flaubert rends the Freethinker. It is unconscious hypocrisy for these great geniuses to tell us that
they merely meant to ridicule grotesque excesses and false
grimaces.

But let us leave aside Don Quixote and Tartufe, who
have no concern here, and return to Homais. What

is he, in Flaubert's eyes ? A stupid inhabitant of a small town who tries to get a little knowledge and to pass judgment on the events of the universe from the back of his little shop. His ambition puts Flaubert in a roar of Homeric laughter. He buries the unhappy man under so much sarcasm that he makes the type ridiculous for years; and we, the readers, overborne by the strong will of the writer, are compelled to become, like him, the enemies of Homais.

But is it so grotesque, this desire of knowledge that animates the poor village chemist in his shop ? Are they merely laughable dolls, all these thousands and thousands of unknown, growing up and dying within their narrow horizons, trying from the depths of their obscurity to catch a few rays of light in their eyes ? Yes, of course; they do not know as much as Flaubert or a university student. Granted, also, that their pride in their bit of half-science is rather solemn. But which of us can flatter himself that he is more than half-learned, and who can swear that he is not vain over his modest lore ? Let us be more charitable toward all inferiorities, even intellectual. From all these millions of Homais scattered over the world, from these millions of Bournisiens, Bouvards, and Pécuchets, from all minds and hearts that have hope, from all these obscure beings, whether they be right or wrong, rises the constant appeal of the planet to the invisible light, science or belief, the eternal Ideal. It is because through generations and over continents Homais disputes, and Bournisien prays, and Bouvard ruins himself, and Pécuchet dies—it is from the " groping " of all these humble folk that, from time to time, are born the Orpheus, the Platos, the Dantes, the Rabelais, the Shakespeares, the Goethes, the Newtons, and the whole long procession of torch-bearers.

That is what Flaubert, the Viking, did not understand.* He could not appreciate the profound law of all human society, which is the solidarity of effort. He had no idea of the infinite hierarchies of minds which the Græco-Latin genius, the most harmonious on this planet, has definitively established. The whole scheme of laws and morals irritated him. He would, like Guiscard's soldiers, have burned Rome because the streets were too narrow.

Let us have the courage to say it—the great writer had at times the brain of a woman. He often lacked the sense of history and politics. He needed the delirium of letters as others needed the delirium of war. He imagined that it was possible to separate art from life and cultivate it apart, far from the human caravan. That is why he had a deplorable influence on all who admired him. He broke the springs of action and fruitful goodness in the souls of the young. He reproduced in developing minds the moral desert of his own mind. He was the most powerful master of modern pessimism.

But, like his ancestors, he loved pomp and plastic beauty—loved them *to the point of delirium*. He was a writer and artist to the death. That is why he raised those marvellous constructions, in different styles, which daze our enchanted senses. But, like the Gothic cathedrals and abbeys of Normandy and England, like the Byzantine or Arab structures of Palermo and Salerno, like all the pages in stone left by the Normans, Flaubert's fine works, rich as they now are in the freshness of their glory, will seem to posterity to be proud and magnificent monuments in a sterile and sumptuous isolation.

* See Note 7 (at end of volume).

PAUL VERLAINE

Away I spin
On the wicked wind,
When it blows.
P. V.

CHAPTER IX

PAUL VERLAINE

I

Am I not born too soon, or late ?
In all the world what can I do ?
And so profound my pains become;
Pray for poor Gaspard, all of you.*

THESE four verses, as moving as a sob, these popular verses which leave a haunting refrain in the heart even more than in the head, and will, like Villon's ballads, live as long as our literature in the memory of men, with their mournful avowal of helplessness, are an admirable summary of the whole of Paul Verlaine's work. They express in a few words, with a radiant simplicity, the whole native nobleness and final decay of this poet of lost genius.

Certainly he was a genius. Few poets in France had more genius than Verlaine. He was born to some great destiny. He bore all the marks of it. Physically, he was as strong and upright as an oak on his native Ardennes. Even in his lamentable decline, when, worn out by vice, misery, and neglect of himself, he limped along the streets of the Latin Quarter, his square shoulders, his proudly erect bearing, and the superb raising of his head, showed the strong ruins of a man who was made to command. Sometimes, in the midst of the trivial, often silly, conversation with which his usual companions whiled away the long and smoky hours at the tables of a café, one would see the aged poet suddenly shake off the

* Translation by Ashmore Wingate, *Sagesse.*

torpor of his heavy-lidded eyes, raise his haughty head, cast a wild and disdainful glance round the band of æsthetes, and then, with outstretched finger, his eye aflame, his lip curled, sweep away with a few decisive syllables the whole mass of folly that had accumulated in the course of the conversation. There was in it something of the thunder of an awakened lion.

At other times when, perchance, curiosity or admiration had gathered round him some groups of writers and sincere artists, whose spirit he loved, the author of *Sagesse* and the *Fêtes galantes* would recover all the seductiveness and vitality of a soul that had seemed moribund. In those moments Verlaine revealed himself to new-comers as both spiritual and profound in his talk, a man of confident learning and of unexpected originality. Then, suddenly, the eye drooped, the head fell heavily on the back of the couch, the wrinkled lips gave out only a few incoherent monosyllables between a pinch of snuff and a sip of absinthe. But the flash of genius had sufficiently illumined this strange man to enable one to see in his far-off destiny the magical signs of a master mind.

Moreover, even if there were no living recollection of Verlaine in the memory of some of us, his work would amply suffice to prove that he was dowered with all the gifts of a true poet. Wealth of imagination, a high instinct for rhythm, spontaneous music of word and phrase, the inspiration of the rising period, brilliant lyricism, novelty in metaphors, inexhaustible variety of style, all the colours and all the shades, an eloquence, at times, like that of a Father of the Church and, at other times, sparkles of Bacchic gaiety, irony and ingenuousness, tenderness and mockery, and, above all, the flight of a swallow or an eagle which enabled him to reach, at one stroke of the wing, the white peaks of the ideal—he had

every gift for enthralling both the crowd and the elect.
At first, indeed, he had not lacked even that painstaking
and deliberate effort that had made a Petrarch, a Rabelais,
or a Goethe—the conscientiousness which he himself
defines imperially:

> The conquest of knowledge, the mastery of toil:
> 'Tis the forehead of Faust sunk low on his hands,
> Perseverance it is, and the power of the will.
> Yes, the holy, eternal, and absolute will.

A marvellous and virile genius he was when he made
his way at the beginning of his career, resplendent with
grace and strength, in the flower-crowned procession of the
new poets. He was a genuine, an indisputable, an irresistible master. What would this son of destiny become ?
A stirrer of ideas, a guide of souls, a renovator of civilisation ? Were we to have a new Vergil, a Dante, an
Orpheus ?

Alas ! to ask the question is the most cruel of ironies.
And, full of pity at so deep a fall, we can, as we approach
his work, only repeat to him the verses he addressed to
himself in some hour of lucid self-examination:

> What hast thou done, who there does sob
>   With endless tears ?
> Say, what didst thou—who there does sob—
>   In thy young years ?
>   ASHMORE WINGATE.

Yes, what had he done ? I knew Paul Verlaine in his
old age, and I am going to recall a few characteristic facts
to show to what depth the poor great man had sunk.

But ought we to speak of the " old age " of a man who
was hardly fifty when he died, the period when the poet is
usually in the full vigour of his rise ? Many others, of the
same age as he, had then, and have retained, a strength of
mind and body of which they could give good account.

Applied to these, the word would be an insult. But Verlaine was old when I saw him: had, doubtless, been very old for a long time, for age, like youth, is not a matter of civil status.

For a man, the decline of life is his reward or his punishment. Those who, in spite of the passions of youth or the combats of maturity, have in their day accomplished the task that was set them; those who, purifying and raising themselves from decade to decade, have gone on intensifying their manly effort after justice, truth, and beauty; those who at each stage took care to be of the age they ought to be, accepting joyously all the fresh labours that the development of their personality brought upon them—those may fearlessly await the inevitable setting of the sun. It will be as beautiful as a harvest evening upon the repose of the well-bound sheaves.

But those who rebel against nature and life, who want to linger in the perturbations of a dead youth, who evade the manly task and miss their destiny, are preparing for themselves a horrible, odious, despairing end. Like aged courtesans and worn-out Don Juans, they pass away in the stale, grey atmosphere of imperfectly extinguished vices and rancid passions, and every recollection that rings in their hearts, recalling the useless past, utters the terrible words: " Too late, too late !"

> In all the world what can I do ?
> And so profound my pains become;
> Pray for poor Gaspard, all of you.

II

I recall scenes the pain of which still moves me. Three visions from those sad years remain ineffaceably in my memory.

Paul Verlaine

One night in 1892 I was going up rue Soufflot with one of the best men I have ever known, the poet Louis Le Cardonnel. We were then incorrigible night-walkers. We could never make up our minds to retire, and we used to accompany each other from door to door, building up, in all the intoxication of our early years, chimerical domes of the future. Suddenly, at the corner of rue Saint-Jacques, we heard shouts, appeals, the noise of a quarrel. There was a row amongst late customers at the door of a wineshop, and the landlord was roughly pushing them out of the place. We went nearer; and whom did we see, furious and gesticulating, in the group? Verlaine himself: Verlaine, our master, our glory, our admiration. We rushed into the crowd, exchanging blows and explanations with the low lot, and we succeeded in getting away the poor poet; the more easily as, to tell the truth, the sound of police coming from the nearest station dissipated the group more effectively than we did. We remained with Verlaine, who was shaking with anger. What had happened? Nothing serious: provocation and bad temper amongst excited drinkers. But in the row Verlaine had lost his large stick; and, as everyone knows, to the end of his life the poet, who was lame, could not walk without the aid of a stick. We took an arm each, and we saw him home, helping his slow and heavy steps.

Oh! that sad, silent, sinister night, with Verlaine, his fury now spent, halting at every step to utter complaints and remorse! All his ingenuous goodness and his irresponsible weakness came out in a mingling of tears and anger. And this was the most glorious poet in France, the most gifted of all who bore the lyre—this human rag which we bore along, and he muttering and storming in turns! I was stirred to the depths of my being. He.

seeing us so deferential, so eager to help, poured out his heart to us:

"What a pity," he said; "what a pity—to see me like this!" Then, suddenly, striking his foot: "I am a pig—a pig, I tell you."

He raged against his absent friends.

"The others—where are they? The cowards! Oh, how lonely I am!"

Le Cardonnel and I, with quivering voices, restored his courage. We reassured him, and we tried to divert him, like a child, with flattering words.

At last we reached his door. It was a furnished house, with a grumbling porter who did not spare insults. We had to push the poet up one flight of stairs after another until we reached his storey. And then, what a spectacle!

Verlaine knocked. The door opened. A horrible woman—ugly, old, dishevelled, in sordid clothes, of rasping voice and hideous mouth—began to pour invectives, in gutter-language, upon the unhappy man. She insulted us also, and accused us of having "made her husband drunk." This harpy—her name was B——was, it seems, the poet's mistress! In a den that was unworthy of a rag-picker, we could have wept with shame to see this man of genius, stretched on a chair, cowed, his lip hanging, trembling with terror before a slut who spat filth at him with every word.

Le Cardonnel and I went away without a word, crushed, choking. In the street we remained silent for a time. We were both filled with horror, and could not exchange our impressions. At last Le Cardonnel gave a start.

"What a disgrace! What a disgrace!" he said.

He spread out his hand in a gesture of repulsion.

"The poor man! What a fate!" I said.

" No, no," said Le Cardonnel. " That isn't life; that isn't work. Oh, what a memory !"

We parted, without daring to say more, in a state of unspeakable grief. Some time afterwards I heard that Le Cardonnel had left Paris; that he had given up literary life, and was about to become a priest. He is now vicar or *curé* of some sunny village in Provence.

The second reminiscence goes back to 1893. It was at one of the banquets of " The Pen," the truculent vanity of which I have described elsewhere. I do not now remember who was the " great man " in the chair. Along the walls, round the tables, were legions of artists chattering. We were just sitting down, and the " dear masters " settled at the more distinguished tables. Amongst these older men were a few well-known officials, rather bewildered at finding themselves in such a place, and some genuine lovers of youth, amongst whom was Stéphane Mallarmé. There were still two chairs empty. Deschamps gave the signal for everybody to be seated, when suddenly the door was noisily opened, and two men came in, arm in arm, stumbling and helping each other. They were Paul Verlaine and Gabriel Vicaire. They were abominably drunk, and were going to the vacant seats at the table of honour. No one would sit until they had taken their places; and the scene was at once comic and lamentable. These two genuine, exquisite poets could scarcely walk. They were laughed at by the whole troop of scribblers and Bohemians who had come to the feast.

" Come on, old man," Vicaire said, " pull yourself together; it's only two yards !"

The quaint expression, just the words of a cheerful drunken man, set the room in a roar. I sat by Georges

177   M

d'Esparbès, and I could not help laughing with him. But I chanced to turn and look at the upper table, and I saw a dumb scene that froze the laugh on my lips and stirred me to the depths of my heart. Behind the illustrious officials, who sniggered as they looked on this humiliating scene, a man, a great poet, one whose life was ever beautiful, turned away to hide a tear. It was Stéphane Mallarmé. I saw at once the deep and sublime sorrow in the heart of this noble servant of the ideal, this man of sinless life and lofty work: in that proud soul that was torn by the laughter of the barbarians and the sight of the fall of his brothers. All my life I will remember the eloquent lesson in human dignity which was given me, in that boisterous hour, by the secret tear of Stéphane Mallarmé.

The last time I saw Paul Verlaine was on a bright autumn morning in 1894. I had gone to the south of France to find a few months of sunshine, enthusiasm, and joy. I had been fortunate enough to spend a few days with Mistral; and the sunny radiation of the great pride of Maillane had given me the support which my wavering youth needed. Full of juvenile intoxication, I told everybody I met the glories of my journey. I met Verlaine at the corner of rue Monge and rue des Écoles. It happened that the author of *Mireille* had spoken very highly to me of the author of *La Bonne Chanson*. The calm, olympian poet of Provence, whose indulgence is not less than his dignity, understood better than any other all that there was of candid genius, of native nobility, and of natural loftiness in the irregular work of the Parisian poet. He liked the vibrant sincerity, the communicative emotion, the ineffable music of the rhythm, the infinite variety of the figures, the unquestionable, radiant good-nature.

" I should very much like to see Verlaine," he had said. So I told Verlaine the compliments I brought from Maillane, and they gave him a delicious joy.

" That good Mistral—what a poet, what a man ! How pleased I am to hear what you tell me."

In spite of its precocious scars, Verlaine's face for a moment took on an air of childish innocence. One would have said that gusts of fresh youth swept up from the depths of his far-off memories. His eyes were sparkling and moist. He made me give him over and over again all the impressions I brought from my pilgrimage in the south. And at each phrase he interrupted me, with his :

" Isn't it fine ? Isn't that real life ?"

Then, gradually, he worked up to a state of indignation against himself, against everybody, against this dreadful Paris :

" What are we people ? What are we—here ? Oh, this cursed city ! What filth to have lived in all that !"

I saw his anger rising. I tried to turn the conversation to talk of trivial things; but he brought me back with his words and his imperious gestures, and at last he fell into violent invectives against himself. And suddenly, sullenly, his eyebrows drawn, without a word of good-bye or explanation, he left me and walked on, muttering :

" Pig, pig !"

His heavy stick beat the pavement, his free arm gesticulated, his bowed head had lost its masterful poise. He walked along alone, swearing, threatening invisible enemies. Then I saw him disappear at the corner of a street, fierce, formidable, sinister, walking straight on without a look at the carriages or pedestrians.

What was taking place in his poor helpless and wounded soul ? What regret of lost youth and lost life stirred up

thus all the memories of his prodigal days ? Was he still
muttering in his heart—but angrily this time:

> In all the world what can I do ?

Was he telling himself that he could never recover the
destiny he had squandered ?

> Oh, naught more can I see,
> All memory's gone
> Of evil and of good.
> Oh, history wan !
> ASHMORE WINGATE.

Was he thinking of the futile efforts he had once made
and had not been able to sustain ?

> For sorrow, and want, and the evil eye
> —Of which I speak not in derision—
> Have given him whom ye saw so high
> The soul of one fading in prison.

Was he still asking himself what he had " done with
his youth " ? I do not know. I never learned. I myself
set out for a healthier life, and I never again saw the
magnificent poor Lélian. Some time afterwards I read
in the *Éclair* a pathetic letter which the sick poet, now
near his end, had written to Mistral, and I recalled that
autumn morning when I saw by Verlaine's gestures how
much acute conscience and devastating remorse there
was in his heart.

And when, after the moving apotheosis of his death,
I piously read his works once more, the works I had
sincerely admired, and of which I still admire the great
poetic beauty, I found again, lingering on every page and
breathing a noxious influence, all the evil with which the
man had been tainted, all the evil that had caused his
thorough helplessness and his final decay. It is this
pernicious fluid, which has perverted and sterilised so

many young minds, that I now propose to study, to show
how much false elegance and real cowardice there is in
enervated literatures which call to their aid the too facile
theory of decadence.

III

The very genius of Verlaine, his lyric gifts, the spon-
taneity of his mind, the frankness of his character, the
limpidity of his ingenuous heart—every quality marked
him out plainly to write sincere work; and his work is,
in fact, verse by verse, the mirror of his own life. Well,
we have seen what his life was. It was the most deplorable fall of a being equipped for beauty, strength,
and creativeness, who, from lack of will and courage,
allowed himself to drift into intellectual weakness, moral
cowardice, the defiling of human dignity, until he ended
miserably in a useless regret of the time he had lost, a
maddening horror of himself, and all the impotence of
remorse.

As he was and lived, so he sang and expressed his
soul. And this sickly soul lingers in his work. It continues to spread the unwholesome influence with which
Verlaine was infected. And there you have, terrible in
its consequences, that undeniable responsibility of the
poet of which I spoke at the outset of these essays.

When an ordinary man, of poor heart and mediocre
mind, with no greatness and no mission, sinks under the
burden of misfortune, and drifts from fall to fall into a
state of helpless resignation, the unhappy man will, after
all, do no harm to any but himself, or, at the most, only
to those immediately round him. But if the man is a
poet, a great poet, a marvellous inventor of rhythm, one
of those privileged beings whose every sensation is trans-
muted into a figure, and every vision translated into

imperishable language, then, by the irresistible prestige of genius, the ideas, the dreams, the desires of this pre-destined mortal infiltrate stealthily into the mind of all who feel his charm, and they provoke there the same mood.

Suppose Verlaine, with all his gifts, had lived the heroic life of an Æschylus, a Dante, or a Cervantes—suppose he had had the calm majesty of a Petrarch or a Goethe, his work would have been suffused with a noble enthusiasm, or would have held the strength of a robust serenity; and we, the readers and admirers, carried away by his lyricism, would have felt in ourselves the happy radiation of his sunlike genius. Instead of that, the gifts being the same, but the courage of the man having failed, it is the nocturnal and pestilential vapours of a vanquished soul that have gradually spread to our deluded souls.

To deny the influence of Verlaine would be to ignore fifteen or twenty years of the literary history of France, to ignore the frame of mind of many of the young even of our own time. Verlaine was, in all the strength of the word, " a master." He is still. He dominated and guided a whole generation; and the prestige of his work continues to act upon minds that are not well prepared to resist it.

But he is a " bad master "; his work is noxious. Like Musset and Baudelaire, he is a " propagator of moral cowardice." He saps energy, kills hope, annihilates virility. In respect of helplessness and evil he completes the work begun by Musset and continued by Baudelaire. The one resigned all heroism to bury himself wholly in love; the other feared life, and sought refuge in dreaming; but Verlaine has not even the seeming aristocracy of the author of *Nights* or the dark pride of the author of the

Flowers of Evil. He is the last step of the ladder by which a man descends when he refuses to do manly work. In him the last spring of the enfeebled will was broken. Poetic individualism, the great blunder of sickly ages, the exaggerated individualism which in the case of his two predecessors still issued in the fumes of an illusory intoxication, reached a sort of comatose condition in his case. It is the refusal to make any kind of struggle, the spirit of indifference to all external dignity—in a word, absolute *decay*—which Verlaine invests in his work with a magical and pernicious beauty.

IV

Perhaps it would be superfluous to give here a few examples of Verlaine's poetry. We should have to quote, one after the other, every verse of the dozen collections. His work has, in fact, in spite of apparent contrasts, a desolating unity. It is the sad drama of his own life; and in his life, even in the days when he seems to be making an effort, he is " the poor Gaspard," who knows no longer " what he came into the world to do." Never was the distress of helplessness, the paralysis of moral weakness, more consistently expressed.

This comedy—or, rather, this lamentable drama of his life—may be divided into five acts, corresponding with five chief moral situations:

1. Fear of struggle, submission to fate, " saturnism."
2. Stupor and oblivion in pleasure and love.
3. Sadness without cause, despair.
4. Attempt to rise, prayer, morbid mysticism.
5. Final fall, renunciation of all effort, definitive abdication.

Did he not from the very outset of his career and his

work place himself under the influence of the planet Saturn ?

> The yellow orb which necromancers love.

Did he not speak of the futility of effort and invoke the higher power of fate ?

> This plan of life was drafted line by line
> By all the logic of a power malign.

Why struggle, then, if one feels oneself the irresponsible toy of a destiny which one cannot control ?

> Away I roam
> On the wicked storm,
>   When it blows.
> First here, then there,
> On the whirling air,
>   Like the straws.

Later, in his most sinister hours, the poet will again plead in excuse this servitude to fate, this futility of struggling against a fore-ordained destiny:

> My life I have squandered; 'tis gone;
> And to all cries of shame and abuse
> I can plead the sufficient excuse
> That 'neath Saturn's dark eye I was born.

It goes so far that in his most cruel trials, in his Belgian prison, he has no cry of revolt either against others or himself. He merely murmurs these lines of tired resignation:

> Of joy in this world I've despaired—
>   Yet am patient still
>   And quite prepared
> For every ill.

But such abandonment of oneself leaves too large a void in the heart, and a man must seek oblivion and numbness elsewhere. Where shall he find them, these entertainments of a feeble soul, if not in love, pleasure, and debauch ? As Musset cried:

> What's life or death to me, my Muse ? I love
> And will grow pale. I love, and I will mourn,
> And give my genius for one well-bought kiss.

As Baudelaire, conscious and deliberate even in his cowardices, said to the woman he desired:

> Can it not be enough, the appearance thou art,
> To bring joy to the soul of *the man who flees truth* ?

So Verlaine, fleeing in his turn the truth that summons him with its daily appeals, asks of love the " drunkenness of the soul " which seems to the dreamers in search of oblivion the great soporific for all our sufferings:

> Hail, sonorous and beautiful kiss ! Divine kiss !
> Delight without peer, drunkenness of the soul !
> For the man who puts lip to thy adorable bowl
> Soaks his being in thy deep, inexhaustible bliss.

This " delight without peer," this " soaking in bliss," begins, in Verlaine's work, with a delicious picture which, in its grace and its luminous frame, has an illusive appearance of strength. It is in the *Fêtes galantes*, where we learn that

> The swains that give the serenade,
> And the fair listeners too,
> Exchange some ponderous conceits
> Beneath the murmuring bough.
> A. WINGATE.

But already, here and there, in this scene of festivity and sweet visions, where we hear the

> . . . thrill of mandolines that down
> The shivering breezes goes,

we see trembling in the poet's avowals that perturbation of heart and sense which follows the inebriation of artificial paradises:

> Dusk fell, Autumn dusk so dubious;
> Dreaming on our arms so low,
> Beauty whispered things that set
> *My soul a-tremble even now.*
>
> A. WINGATE.

To the shivering " breezes " of the *Fêtes galantes* succeeds the more nervous love of *La Bonne Chanson,* in which the poet heard the first whisperings of remorse :

> As in deep woods, in love we're lost and gone :
> Each heart a tender peace round either throws ;
> Two nightingales, at dusk we'll sing alone.
>
> A. WINGATE.

Even in this wilful isolation, however, destiny or " Fate " still haunts the fugitive from life :

> We shall not trouble what Fate hath destined
> For us, we'll march with an unfaltering foot.
>
> A. WINGATE.

But, alas ! who can exorcise what Baudelaire calls " the knowing Ideal " ?   Neither the " drunkenness of the soul " in kisses, nor the " ponderous conceits of the fair listeners," nor the " dark woods " in which they seek refuge from the world, can prevent what the other great poet of the dream called " the operation of avenging mystery." And the " good song " soon gives place to the mournful air of the *Romances sans paroles :*

> This little soul which doth lament
> Itself in such a sleepy plaint,
> It is our own, is it not so ?
>
> A. WINGATE.

It is certainly his, for he returns to it in still more dolorous verses :

> My heart and soul that are aflame
> Are but a kind of double eye,
> Through which, alas ! comes tremblingly
> That air on every lyre the same.*

---

* Modified from Wingate, who mistakenly makes the verse joyous.

Then the third act begins, the inevitable sadness, the despairing *lamento* of helplessness:

> Oh, the sky was so blue, and the hope was so high !
> —Now poor hope on bruised wing rises to the black sky !

And this:

> O sad, sad was this soul of mine,
>   And all, all for a woman's sake;
> Nor am I salved, although my heart
>   Did of itself an exile make.
>   A. WINGATE.

And in that mood of despair sadness invades the heart, and the poet knows no longer what the cause of all his trouble is:

> He weeps for no reason
> In his disheartened heart.
> What, was there no treason ?
> The tears have no reason.
>
> 'Tis the worst kind of fate
> When one knows not even why,
> Without love, without hate,
> The heart finds not its mate.

This bitter lament over the difficulty of finding joy poor Verlaine was to repeat all his life, on every possible note.   It is a sort of *leit motiv* of his work:

> A sleep black and deep
> Dully falls on my life.
> Dear hope, do thou sleep;
> Desire, cease thy strife.

And again:

> I cannot tell why
> My spirit should be
> So foolish and anxious as she roams the sea.
> Whatever to me
> Was dear seems to fly.
> My love scatters sadly.   In vain I ask why ?

It is useless for him in these sombre days to try to recover the intoxication of his lost loves:

> My torturer, Time, to kill thee my soul moves
> Far away to the fragrant days of my chaste loves,
> And my joy and my shame I nurse to the sweet sound
> Of kissing her hand. . . .

The illusion is too poor. The poet's heart is " weak and foolish ":

> He takes ship, full of hope, for the island of dreams,
> But he finds naught but tears that flow gently in streams
> Which he loves, and black brooding and hours of despair.
> He returns . . .

And at last he breaks out against everything—against himself, fate, and woman:

> Of a truth I have suffered enough,
> Ever spurred by the hounds like a wolf
> That must fly every day to new place,
> With no den and no rest,
> Ever haunted and pressed,
> Driven on by the whole human race.

Will he never find the refuge that he seeks, this " hunted wolf," " driven on " by sadness and remorse ?

Yes. He finds it for a moment. At least, he thinks that he has found it—in mysticism.

V

Much has been said about Verlaine's mysticism. Many have spoken highly of the supposed evolution of the poet, raising himself to " the pure light of the Christian faith " after the trials and errors of his youth. I have heard devout Catholics say that the author of *Sagesse* was a great Christian poet; if not the greatest, the only, Christian poet. Others saw in him the restorer of

mysticism in France. I have been present at very
learned lectures in psychic science, at which some of
Verlaine's sonnets were read as models of spiritual purity.
I am incompetent, I admit, to discuss questions of
religious doctrine with theologians and *magi;* yet I think
that these learned critics are mistaken. In default of
special light, I have for my guidance in this study, as
a basis of comparison, some knowledge of other poets
and writers whose Christian faith was indisputable, such
as Dante, Bossuet, and Lamartine; and I am certainly
not wrong in thinking that in their prayers and invocations
there is an entirely different accent from that of poor
Verlaine. In any case, we are quite certain of one thing
—that books like *Sagesse* and *Amour* do not mean either
a change or an exception in Verlaine's work. They are
completely bound up with all the others. They are a
logical outcome of the others. They have the same
general tone. They round off the lamentable unity of
this lost life. They are simply one act, along with others,
of this painful drama. It is the attempt of a despairing
man to find salvation: a useless attempt, moreover,
because the poet will show just the same moral inertia
here as elsewhere.

Certainly there is no doubt about the sincerity of his
conversion. His faith is profound. The prayers issue
from his heart. Verlaine is incapable of hypocrisy, either
in good or evil. But there is no force in his faith. It
does nothing . It consists only in weeping over himself,
in unceasing repentance, without the least attempt to
rise.

> God of the lowly ! Save this child of wrath;

he cries. And he calls upon God to behold his weakness,
and confesses his helplessness:

> Thou, God of peace, of joy, of happiness,
> All my dark fears, my pain, my ignorance,
> Thou, God of peace, of joy, of happiness,
> Thou knowest all, Thou knowest all;
> And that no weaker soul than mine doth live,
> Thou knowest all, Thou knowest all;
> But what I have, O God, to You I give.

What he " has," what he " gives," is just the avowal of his weakness, the declaration of his humility. Read, for instance, the famous sonnets, so beautifully lyrical, in which the poet commemorates his surrender to Jesus:

> My God has said: My son, thou shalt love Me. Behold
> My piercèd side, My heart that gives out rays and blood.

Can you see anything else in it than the thought which is summed up in these twelve syllables:

> Unworthy am I, but Your clemency I know ?

One feels that, even in the sincerity of prayer, Verlaine has no will. His mysticism is merely a refuge from life. He casts himself into the arms of the Church much as vagabonds and swashbucklers once sought protection in monasteries. It is not with an idea of bettering his life; it is to escape the punishment that threatens.

The whole " wisdom " of the poet may be summed up in these words—Catholic, I admit, but far from heroically Catholic: " Lord, I am a very wicked child, and I fear I am unable to change. But I love You so much, Lord, and I feel so humble a contrition, that, surely, You will let me off."

It seems that this humility is the most precious of Christian virtues, and that it suffices. I am prepared to believe it; and, not knowing the secrets of the Lord, I must grant that it is enough. But the rest of us, poor mortals, and very imperfect mortals, as we are, have some reason not to find it enough. It is very fine to be

a humble sinner; but a little less humility and a little
more manly courage would give us more joy in this frail
world. I am more or less Christian, but, even if it brings
upon me a charge of heresy, I say that I prefer an un-
believer or an atheist who strives for truth and moral
beauty to a servant of God who continues to soil himself
with filth while uttering his edifying professions of
repentance. To pray is good: to act is, perhaps, better.

And in a book which is certainly as Christian as *Sagesse*,
the *Imitation of Christ*, I find this manly maxim, so
different from Verlaine's enervated groans:

> It is a greater thing to resist one's vices and one's passions
> than to pour out one's sweat in corporal works.

Later, in the same book, we read:

> You will make progress only in proportion to the violence that
> you do to yourself.

And if we wish to hear the accents of genuine mystic
poetry, let us turn to Dante's *Paradiso*, and we shall see
how neither humility nor prayer dispenses a man from
having an heroic soul:

> *O divina virtù, se mi ti presti*
> *Tanto che l' ombra del beato regno*
> *Segnata nel mio capo io manifesti,*
>
> *Venir vedra' mi al tuo diletto legno,*
> *E coronarmi allor di quelle foglie,*
> *Che la materia e tu mi farai degno.*
> (Canto Primo.)

Is Lamartine less Christian than Verlaine ? He says:

> Let us witness to Christ by the light of our lives;
> For the least of our virtues more the impious drives
> Than the martyr's pure blood.

Compare the sort of religious terror that rules in
Sagesse with the active strength that exhales from
Lamartine's *Harmonies*. The one says:

> Tender, dear humility,
> Water thou my charity,
> Steep it in thy waters sweet,
> That my heart may no more beat,
> Till a pious death draws near.

One would say that he sees nothing in faith but in-activity and silence. Lamartine draws from it the will to say and to accomplish everything:

> O may I, spirit strong,
> Full of promise to the laden,
> In thy shadow breathe a song
> Like a harp in heaven !
> Grant that I, when the words on my lips cold expire,
> Be a voice for all time in thy heavenly choir.

Then you have, five centuries later, the same virile cry that Dante raised at the gates of Paradise:

> *Entra nel petto mio, e spira tue. . .*

Those are the genuine, the noble, mystics; and, what-ever one may think of religious inspiration in itself, whether one be a believer or an atheist, there is one thing on which all agree—the faith which inspires poets with enthusiasm and energy is the only living faith. The other is but a babbling of sacristans. It gives neither help nor comfort. Verlaine is as demoralising in his prayers as in his love-songs. For the rest, we know well, from the sequel, how little help he got from this false mysticism. In spite of this movement toward the light, the last act of his life and his work was even more deplorable than the rest. He went from fall to fall, finally abdicating all moral beauty, defiling even the flower of his poetic genius in the degradations of *Jadis et naguère* and the insanities of *Parallèlement*. No doubt, we occasionally still find the admirable lyric note of *Sagesse*, the marvellous picturesqueness of the *Fêtes galantes ;* but the soul becomes weaker and weaker, the poetry poorer and poorer, until at last we get these painful confessions of depravation:

> Prince or princess, slave of virtue or vice.
> Whoever doth chide me, be he high or low,
> Poet of fame or announcer of bliss,
> Know that I am the peer of the fiery Sappho.

We will go no farther. Had he not in his hidden soul the naïveness of a savage child ? He knew not the evil that he did to himself and others. But he did it. Let us, all the same, pity him and love him. Let us recall with deferential compassion the " dolorous way " of this failure. Let us pray for the poor Gaspard. But we have a right to defend ourselves against the contagion: to say that the great poet Verlaine, born to realise a high destiny, endowed to accomplish a work of beauty and strength, stopped at the first inns on his journey and failed in his mission.

VI

I know the excuses that are made. He was " an artist," we are told, and as such his only function in the world was to give expression to his soul as it was. Further, he was a poet of decadence; and it is not his fault if, in his poems, he was a mirror of the decadence amidst which he lived.

I will not linger to refute the theory of art for art's sake. Nowadays it has rather the air of an ancient story. I do not know a single writer worthy of the name who now amuses himself by expounding it in some prehistoric chamber. Everybody who thinks and lives long ago gave up these follies of women and eunuchs.

But I should like to say a word about this decadence

theory, as it is still discussed occasionally, in connection with Baudelaire, Verlaine, and other morbid contemporaries.

If we believe certain psychologists, we are living in a decomposing environment, morbid, " deliquescent "— to use a word that has become famous—and therefore the artist is bound to make himself the interpreter of this putrefaction. I believe that M. Paul Bourget has expounded this theory in his *Essais de psychologie contemporaine*, precisely in connection with Baudelaire. As to Verlaine, it is well known that he himself claimed the title " decadent," and that his disciples considered it an honour.

A singular aberration, certainly ! A strange conception of the poet's function ! Decadence of what, or of whom ? Of the world ? Of mankind ? Where do you find it ? On every hand new peoples arise, civilisations are founded, new forces grow stronger. There was never before so much movement on the earth. Decadence of France ? What do we know about it ? Where is there irrefutable proof of it ? Has France not perpetually had its rises and falls ?

However, not to prolong the discussion, let us admit this decadence. Let us suppose for a moment that we live in a decrepit age. How does that justify the work of morbid poets ? Why must we utter cries of despair and cowardice ? Is it all over with the land and its history ? Are there not invariably such things as renaissances ? Have we not learned the serene law of resuscitated and rejuvenated peoples ? The word "decadence" always stupefies us, because our classic mind is full of Roman memories. But a decadence like that of Rome, when the whole world seemed to die simultaneously, is an event that will never be repeated on this planet.

Paul Verlaine

The nervousness of the last Latin and Greek poets would in our time be a piece of stupidity or ignorance. We have seen other instances of partial decay; and we have seen how genuine and great poets have behaved therein.

Was not Florence in Dante's time, and Rome in Petrarch's, in a desperate condition ? Did not these noble geniuses and fine citizens see slowly perishing under their eyes the frame of their country, the object of their deepest affection ? Think of the sad end of the exiled Florentine in the house of his friend Cane Grande della Scala; and remember the desolate condition of Rome at the time when Petrarch's eyes were closing. These two great men died in an atmosphere of public calamity. Both saw the failure of their hope of the resuscitation of Italy: a hope for which they had written and wrought. If any poets ever lived in the twilight of a decadence, it was these illustrious Italians.

Did they abandon their task ? Did they abandon themselves to groans of despair and relax into devotion to purely individualist work ? Did they utter the "What does it matter ?" of the weak ? Never. To the day of their death they behaved like citizens and men. And when at length the Renaissance came, their work rose up once more, the victorious herald of glories yet to come.

That was because they had understood the poet's mission as guide of souls; because they knew that it was his duty to grow yet more in strength and courage when everything seems to sink around him. Decadence, do you say ? It is only another reason why the torch-bearer must lift higher still the light he has to spread.

It is easy to say: "I am the mirror of my age." A conscious and responsible being a mirror ! Does the turpitude of others justify decay in us, especially when destiny calls us to be the guides of the straying flock ?

No. The truth is that there are strong hearts and there are faint hearts. Villon lived in an age of robust power, under the most victorious of kings. Yet he was a poor man, though a great poet. So was Verlaine, in our own time: this supposed decadence had nothing to do with it. There are noble souls—and the others; that is the whole truth. There are those who revolve about their own miserable self, weeping and dreaming of futile things, mourning lost lives and dying of languor. And there are those who feel the beauty of their mission; who know that the poet has charge of souls, and that one's own, considered apart, is nothing to humanity. In two words, there is such a thing as individualist poetry, the poetry of unfinished poets, and human poetry—that of Homer, and Vergil, and Dante, and Cervantes, and Corneille, and Shakespeare, and Goethe, and Lamartine, and Hugo, and all the souls whom one of them calls

Quique pii vates et Phœbo digna locuti.

These alone do glorious work.

ÉMILE ZOLA

You do not know what you want to do.
I do not know what you want to do.
What you want to do, I will do.
From a speech of Zola to the Symbolists, 1891.

CHAPTER X
EMILE ZOLA

I

I HAVE not only admiration, but respect, for the memory of Émile Zola. I do not think there is any man in French literature, not even excepting Hugo and Renan, who had a higher and more superb idea of the duty of a writer. He was, in the gigantic effort of his ardent genius, always brave, strong, and generous. He had in the highest degree the solid virtues which constitute character; the will which shrinks not from work; the energy which accomplishes it; the courage which flings itself against obstacles; the tenacity which holds out against opposing forces; the patience which disdains defeat; the faith which sustains a man until the victory is won. Above all, he had pride in his part: a pride so robust, so lofty, so valiant that it must be an example and an encouragement for every man who sets out to write with any nobleness.

Zola was, all his life, the firmest and most complete realisation in the nineteenth century of what a writer ought to be in the midst of the turmoil of social life, and what he will be in the future. Deliberately, in accordance with a firm and admirable plan, he was, and wished to be, wholly and entirely a writer; and as writer alone he tried to shake the world, and did in fact shake it.

The others strove to get official places in the social hierarchy. Lamartine and Chateaubriand were ambassadors and ministers; Victor Hugo, very respectful to established situations, was a peer of France, a Senator, a Grand Cross, and it is said that he was a little distressed that he was not invited to play a great part in the political world; Renan occupied official positions, and confesses himself, naïvely, that he had weaknesses which were rather puerile for so great a mind. " The only two ambitions I ever professed," he says in his *Souvenirs de jeunesse*, " the Institut and the Collège de France, were gratified." And the malicious author of *Caliban* does not add that he had a third ambition—to enter the Senate—which was not gratified, to his lasting distress. As to Balzac, in spite of his fine work as a writer and the courageous life of struggle he sustained so untiringly, pen in hand, it is no longer a secret that he had always dreamed of escaping from literature and shining in a high social position; that he had in him that soul of a " careerist " which he has so magnificently exhibited to the world in the person of his favourite hero, Rastignac.

In reality, there was no writer of the nineteenth century who dared to liberate literature from the state of slavery in which it had been for centuries in relation to every form of power. No one dared proclaim its absolute independence, the supremacy of its influence, its royal power. Flaubert was content to keep it apart, far from every movement, in a fixed ivory tower. Zola was the first to vindicate the active and effective greatness of the writer, freed from every attachment to public forces, above power, above the crowd, obeying only his own conscience, strong in his genius alone. No one has more loftily proclaimed " a concern for the dignity of letters."

II

Read again, you young men who are in a hurry to shine in the world, you who are tormented with impatience about your future, and you, also, who groan over the tardiness of human glory—read the critical works of Zola: those steaming pages of unrelenting assault, reverberating with clarion blasts, lit by the lightning of a radiant struggle. Read again *Mes haines*, the *Roman expérimental*, *Documents littéraires, Une Campagne*—read the whole. You will not like the ideas, perhaps; some will seem out of date. What does it matter? Behind the controversial and perhaps disputable ideas there is something that is absolutely beautiful, that forces admiration. It is the robust temperament, the intrepid courage of the man.

What a noble and pure ardour for the triumph of human thought there must have been in the man who wrote: " Would that genius were solely the agent of future ages "! With what spirit he attacks and demolishes the fools, the pedants, and the knaves of the literary world ! What chivalrous defiance constantly hurled at those who, in his view, unjustly cling to a power they have usurped ! Nothing can stop him: neither the established situation, nor the power of his opponents, nor the coalition of the forces against him. Some of these articles raised the entire Press against him. He was expelled from one paper for daring to say what he thought. He was insulted, libelled, charged with vile things. Yet, still covered with the mud flung at him, he returned always to the battle, never tired, never beaten, seeking nothing but the triumph of letters.

How splendid is the anger that breaks from him in this passage:

> Hatred is holy. It is the indignation of strong and powerful hearts, the militant disdain of those who resent mediocrity and folly. To hate is to love, to feel one's heart warm and generous, to live largely on contempt of shameful and beastly things. Hate consoles: hate does justice: hate makes a man great.
>
> I have felt myself younger and more courageous after each of my revolts against the platitudes of my age. I made hatred and pride my two guests. I took pleasure in isolation, and, in my isolation, hating whatever hurt justice and truth.

He was twenty-five years old when he wrote these lines, but he remained the same all his life: ardent, impassioned, generous. All his anger came from the sincerity of his heart. His most violent, even his most unjust, attacks never had an unworthy motive. He said:

> It was always the baseness and beastliness of men that set my heart aflame.

The turpitudes of servile souls and the follies of mediocre minds hurt him as if he had been personally wounded. But his most splendid anger is that which he shows in presence of the sterile politicians and men of blatant ambition who want to lower and soil the high function of literature. On these occasions Zola becomes a sort of knight of the written thought, and his accent, in the end, rises to the lyrical pitch of the prophets. He said:

> My anger is there, in the proliferation of these parasites, in the stupefying noise they make, in the shameful spectacle of a great people eaten up by men without any talent whatever, anxious only to satisfy the terrible hunger of their low ambition. . . . *That is why I have so loudly demanded the independence of letters.* Literature alone reigns for ever. It is absolute, while politics is relative. In our troubled times politicians, thanks to the confusion of the nation, assume a great and unwholesome importance which must be fought. These puppets of an hour, these generally unconscious tools of some accident that they had not foreseen, must be reduced

to their proper proportions, if the country is not to be led astray by their performances. No, they are not everything. Theirs is not the epoch: it belongs to the scholars and writers. That is the cry I would like to raise above the turmoil of our political muddles. Your noise will cease: our works will live. You are nothing: we are everything. And if I were the only man in the world to cry it aloud, I should say it with full confidence in the loftiness of my task and in your final extinction.

Another time, in *La Haine de la littérature*, he again attacks the politicians and vindicates *the priority of letters*:

There is the hospital, the menagerie; and so much the worse if it makes people angry, for I have no words strong enough for my revolt. Yes, I am disgusted by such a parade of bad and bestial ambitions. Show me a scrofulous man, a cretin, an imperfectly developed brain, and you have the stuff of a politician. . . . When a man has failed in everything, when he has been a mediocre lawyer, a mediocre journalist, a mediocre man from head to foot, politics gets hold of him and makes him as good a minister as the others, ruling as a more or less modest *parvenu* over the intelligence of France. Those are the facts.

My God, the facts are still tolerated, for hardly a day passes without something equally strange. The observer becomes accustomed to do nothing but smile. But what fires my heart is when these people affect to despise and protect *us*. We are only writers. We hardly count. They limit our place in the sun. They put us at the foot of the table. Well, gentlemen, now that we understand the situation, we intend to be first: to have the whole table and the whole of the sun. You shall know that a single page written by a great writer is more important to the race than a whole year of your ant-hill fussiness. You make history, it is true; but we make it with you, and more than you, for it is owing to us that it is enduring. Your life, as a rule, is spent in the infinite pettiness of a personal ambition from which the nation derives no practical service; but our works, of their very nature, contribute to the civilisation of the world. For the rest, see how rapidly you are dying. Read some history of the last years of the Restoration, for instance, and ask yourselves what has become of so many political battles and so much eloquence. Only one thing remains to-day, after fifty years: the great literary development of the period, the romanticism whose leaders have remained illustrious while the statesmen have dropped out of the public memory. Understand, you little men who make so much noise, it is *we* who live, and who award immortality. We must say it boldly. Literature is at the top, with science. Politics comes afterwards, much lower, amongst the relative elements of human affairs.

This idea of the supremacy of letters and science is a favourite with him. He proclaims it and vindicates it repeatedly. In another place he says:

Science and letters alone are certitudes. They have time and space before them. *If some man must constantly repeat this, I have undertaken the part and will never drop it.*

What spirit in these lofty claims ! Zola was often accused of pride, and he defended himself with thrilling eloquence against the charge of individual pride:

Alas ! I have too strong a critical sense. I should like to be convinced that I am the first man of my age. The writer who reaches this stage of hypertrophy of personality lives in a superb serenity. He makes speeches to himself before a mirror. He becomes a god. But, to my sorrow, I still weep with rage over my manuscripts. I call myself an idiot a score of times every morning. I never publish a book without thinking it inferior to its predecessors.

But there is another sort of pride, and this he claims, because it is legitimate and worthy. It is what we all ought to have, and Zola had in the highest degree. It is the collective pride of literary work: the necessary pride of the thinker who is to stir the consciences of men. As Zola says, speaking again of politics:

All that will pass away, and we will remain. That is what gives us a little pride. *Pride, whatever be said of it, is health for such a debased age as ours.*

A fine phrase, and proof of a great heart ! Yes, the dignity of letters was raised by the man who loudly proclaimed the right and the *duty* of the writer to depend on none but himself, to ask nothing of the public authorities, and offer his work to his country and demand nothing in

return. Listen to the admirable advice he gives to young
men in *L'Argent dans la littérature*. After showing that
money earned by the writer's labour is a legitimate profit
on his work which has freed him from any humiliating
protection, and has turned the former dependent of the
court and clown of the antechamber into a free citizen,
a man relying on none but himself, Zola eloquently
concludes:

> Work—everything lies in that. Rely on none but yourselves.
> Tell yourself that if you have talent, it will open to you the most
> firmly closed doors, and will set you as high as you deserve to rise.
> Above all, refuse any advantages from public officials, and *never
> ask the protection of the State ; for that would be to abandon your
> manliness.* The great law of life is struggle. No one owes you
> anything. You will inevitably triumph if you are a force, and,
> if you fail, do not complain, for it is just.

Yes, proud, dignified, noble—such was Émile Zola,
beyond dispute. And if he had not, near the end, shown
a deplorable weakness which disturbs a little the superb
frame of his life of energy and will, his career would be the
most perfect model we could recommend to the writers of
the future.

III

It is difficult to understand by what aberration or
failure the vigorous controversialist of *Une Campagne*
could at the height of his triumph so far forget the attitude of his early and his mature years as to demand an
official decoration and seek a chair in the Academy.

That was, in my opinion, Zola's great fault: the defect
of his life, which is otherwise so noble: the clay portion of
his proud pedestal. There are superficial folk who will
ask why I make so much of social formalities that are,
perhaps, rather vain, but have become so common that

everybody observes them just as he complies with the fashion. They will be surprised, especially, that I insist on these petty ambitions on the part of Zola, when I have not said a word about them in speaking of the other masters. They will quote the examples of distinguished poets whom I often praise, such as Goethe, Lamartine, or Victor Hugo, who were decked out with crosses and all sorts of honours.

I reply that these " social formalities," trivial as they may have been for Zola's predecessors, are of primary importance in the case of the author of *Une Campagne*. In their case it was casual; in his a revelation of his temperament. And his error in this respect will help us to discover the weak point in his genius.

Zola's position in face of official dignities was not the same as that of writers before his time. There were differences in the age and the environment; and the original speculator of *L'Argent dans la littérature* knew this better than any, because he had himself described them with luminous eloquence. He had shown how the social dignity of the writer had grown from the Renaissance to modern times.

Malherbe had been pensioned by Marie de Medicis. Corneille and Molière were supported by Colbert. La Bruyère was in the pay of the Prince de Condé. This position of dependence did not prevent such noble writers from showing the pride of their souls, and no one would dream of reproaching them with the state of servitude in which they lived. They merely submitted to the exigencies of the time. But if an able writer of our day accepted this state of domestic slavery, he would be base and contemptible. Why ? Because manners have changed, and the moral and material position of writers has been more and more emancipated and improved.

It is the same in regard to official dignities. Probably
if there appeared in our time a great mind, a man like
Goethe, he would despise vulgar honours, and sit enthroned
above nations and governments in his own radiant, sun-
like beauty. Such a domination was impossible in the
eighteenth century, in the small courts of Federal
Germany. Men had scarcely emerged from the state of
subjection in which the poet had been in the reign of
Louis XIV. and his imitators. When he became an important personage and a friend of the Grand Duke Karl
August, Goethe raised the dignity of literature and prepared the way for the coming supremacy of the thinker.
Moreover, the great olympian of Weimar, born of wealthy
parents, destined to the highest positions, was in his
natural environment in " the Athens of the north."
A solitary attitude, apart from the court and the academies, would at that time have been misunderstood, and
therefore contrary to the perfect serenity of Goethe and
harmful to the influence of his genius.

As to Lamartine and Hugo, their birth and position
marked them out plainly for public honours. The one,
born in the nobility, educated to shine in a diplomatic
career, regarded poetry only as the refined pastime of a
man of action. The other, the son of a general, reared in
a literary atmosphere, could not conceive the triumph of
his school complete unless it was consecrated by academic
dignities. Moreover, people were then just issuing from
the Imperial period, when social pomp had been restored
with the splendour which the dominating genius of
Napoleon gave to all his actions. In a word, until the
time of Zola no distinguished poet could dream of breaking
with the institutions which awarded honours.

Émile Zola, on the other hand, had not the excuse of
environment, birth, and accepted traditions. Robust

plebeian, forging ahead apart from any help or protection, he was a self-made man. He came at the time when the material position of writers emancipated them for ever from every kind of slavery. It was the time when the Press enabled its contributors to earn their daily bread by their own labour: the time when the bookshop and the theatre gave ease, and often fortune, to gifted writers. Who knew better, and acclaimed more loudly, than Zola these indisputable advantages? What a splendid opportunity it was for a strong man to free literature from the last bond that held it to the social hierarchy, to lift it above the ruts, the salons, the banquets, the ministers, the academies, to proclaim, by word and example, the absolute independence, the unchallengeable superiority, of the written thought!

Zola could do it, and ought to have done it. He ought, because, so far from being ignorant of this new duty of a vigorous genius, he had himself formulated, in decisive terms, the mission of the literary emancipator.

Was it not he who proudly wrote: " Never ask the protection of the State "? Was it not he who hurled at the orpheonists of literature this rude message: " I am nothing—not even a Bachelor of Letters: I belong to nothing—not even the Society of Men of Letters "? It was he also who defined the task of an author of sound character in maxims which ought to be written in letters of gold on the walls of every study:

All that the Government can do for us is to give us absolute freedom. At present the highest idea we have of a writer is a free man who needs to flatter none; who owes his life, his talent, and his glory to himself alone: giving himself to his country and asking nothing in return.

As to the Academy, no man ever spoke of it more severely and more justly. No one ever saw better its actual uselessness, or better described its vain decrepitude:

> The Academy also has ceased to exist: I mean, as a force and an influence in literature. Its chairs are still eagerly coveted, just as, from the vanity that is in all of us, decorations are still coveted. But it no longer lays down the law. It is no longer an authority on our language. The literary prizes it distributes count for nothing with the public. They generally go to mediocrities. They have no meaning, as they do not indicate or encourage any movement. . . . It is not merely useless; it is a hindrance. It is vain and weak enough to open its arms to the men it had at first tried to devour. Such an institution cannot count for anything in the life of a nation. It has no meaning, no action, no results. . . . I repeat, its place in our literature is nothing at all. It is a halo of the past.

That was what Zola said in the full glory of his conscious manhood. And the day came when he accepted, even demanded, an official decoration from the French Government. He even sought a chair in this Academy which is "nothing at all," which he justly described as a mere "halo of the past." What, after such assaults to make such a retreat? It was more than a defeat; it was a surrender. It was the disavowal of a life of struggle for the supremacy of letters and the dignity of the writer. Such a fault in such a life is enormous. It destroys the balance and harmony.

IV

Did his character weaken, as has been generally supposed? Did Zola, as he grew older, lose his virile energy? Or, rather, did he, in the hour of victory, in the charm of the rest he had won, come to feel that "pressure of vanity that is in all of us," to use his own words? It seems that there are well-informed people who speak of some feminine influence to which the blunt author of *Mes haines* eventually yielded. Woman is, indeed, a terrible forger of chains. Even when she prides herself on having a free spirit, she is bound to the world by the insidious threads of vanity, and all real pride seems to her an insult to her power. It is possible that even the great and good Zola may, in his carelessness, have been caught in the subtle snare of feminine suggestion.

However that may be, I do not admit any failure of his moral sense. It would be too culpable in such a man. It would point to some sort of baseness; and I find nothing of the kind in Zola. It would prove that the fervour of his convictions was not sincere; and that would be false. Until the last day of his life he gave proof of energy, pride, and independence. No, it was neither from weakness nor vanity that he gave the lie to his ideas. It is not his character, but his grasp of life, that we must impugn.

It is necessary to insist on this point, because here we are going to find the chief defect of his genius; and this defect will enable us to assign the proportion of morbid perturbation and dark influence that came from Zola's work and made this powerful and upright writer a " bad master," in spite of his solid virtues.

Zola never saw things on a high level. He lacked that aristocracy of spirit which is needed by any who would guide men and stir their thoughts. He had not the requisite disdain of contingencies. Throwing himself fierily into the fight, he never kept quite clear of the smoke. Even in his bravest and most disinterested actions he often exhibited a quite useless and childish ardour. He made the mistake of generals who rush furiously to every part of the battle and in the end lose sight of it as a whole. The actual swept him away in its whirlpool. He believed in ephemeral things and accidental facts. How often did he not mistake a mole-hill for a mountain that was to be scaled, and raise his giant arms to fight a dwarf! He always lacked serenity, and sometimes clearness of mind.

For instance, in regard to decorations and academies he was the victim of an exaggerated respect, of the sort of fetichism which he had for his time. He waged an implacable and valiant battle, and he gained the victory, bearing along with him all who worked with him. But in all good faith, he thought that his victory required some sort of sanction. He wanted official consecration, if not for himself, at least for his ideas and his troops. What sort of consecration could he expect other than that which already existed in the field of struggle? All round him he bumped against dignities and academic chairs. He now demanded, as tokens of his success, the dignities and honours which he had despised.* That was his mistake.

The argument he used is well known:

If the decoration exists, I ought to have it. If there is an Academy, I ought to belong to it.

This was childish and sophistical. There is no doubt about Zola's sincerity, but what ingenuousness! It is by just such arguments that all doomed institutions have their life prolonged, and a semblance of greatness is given to all the servilities of fashion. " This is a foolish and useless thing—but, as it exists, I ought to have it." Could he not see that these words, prompted by his generous and combative pride, would serve equally to excuse the low tricks and platitudes of every "careerist"? And how insipid! What an unexpected reversal of the victory he had won!

Was it really that which he set out to gain when he

* See Note 8 (at end of volume).

proclaimed the priority of letters ? Was that all he
found to make clear the supremacy of the writer ?
Instead of raising himself above men, above the ruts, the
vanities, and the hierarchies, high up on the hill of light,
this torch-bearer, this guide of the race, humbly entered
the rank and file. He received a corporal's stripe by way
of consecration. Because, when he allowed himself to
be nominated for the Legion of Honour, he deliberately
took his place below every adventurer who had the Grand
Cross When he sought votes in the Academy, he not
only bowed down to an institution that he had described
as moribund, but he—the creator of worlds, the thinker—
suffered himself to be judged and classified by some drawing-room fop, to be elected by means of the influence
of some society woman. Was that the great victory of
letters ? Was this degrading surrender to be the end of
the heroic effort sustained during thirty years of battle ?
How came he thus to betray both himself and us ?

He saw well in the last act of his life, which was so
splendid and so courageous, whatever one may think of
that much discussed affair, that there was no need to be
laden with honours and dignities to shake the world.
When he had such influence as to divide the whole
French nation into those who were for him and those
who were against him, it was not because he wore a red
rosette or because he was President of the Society of Men
of Letters. It was because he was Zola, and solely
because he was Zola. It was because he had written his
famous works; because his talent broke out in a magnificent fighting style; because he spread the inspiration
and the empire of genius. At that moment he did indeed prove, with all his strength, " the priority of letters."
This man, without mandate, without titles or any othei
apparatus, struggling alone against courts, ministers,

and constituted powers, and holding them in check, rose to an epic greatness. Whether or no one likes his ideas, and even if one thinks that he made too much of trivial quarrels, his strong way extorted admiration. For any man who regards things from a high level, without passion, with the serene impartiality of history, this was really the triumph of thought over force; and it was magnificent.

Unhappily, this courageous and disinterested conduct does not palliate the effect of Zola's great weakness. Palliate? The truth is that the prestige which his last public act gave him in Europe and in the literary world only made more injurious the influence of his betrayal of his own ideas.

This man of genius and character, whose teaching and example could have saved literature from all the pettiness of the senile hierarchies, led, by his failure, to a fresh outpour of vanity and intrigue. Had he remained faithful to the lofty maxims of *Une Campagne* and the *Roman expérimental*, he would have compelled all who came after him to adopt his attitude of pride, if only from human respect. And gradually literature would have been purified of every servile element, as public morality improved. Instead of that, what excuse did he not provide for all men of false pride, all who were eager to be in the public eye? What a rush once more for the glitter of social vanities! How the supposed independent men hastened to cover themselves with decorations! They were quite justified in seeking them, as Zola had done so. Never did literature exhibit so much baseness and servility: contests, prizes, medals, palms, and crosses everywhere. Modern literature is now one vast agricultural show; and it is the " revolutionaries " who set the example. Every " rebel " is a laureate in the academic games. Every " anarchist " belongs to the Legion of

Honour. Of the "free spirits," the "apostles of the people," those who do not aspire to the French Academy seek the Maison Goncourt: which is much the same thing. That is where we have got to in 1904, a quarter of a century after *L'Assommoir!*

Who will perform the act of courage needed to deliver and restore us which Zola failed to perform after promising it in his splendid manhood ? Who will be strong enough, high enough above public opinion, to raise once more the dignity of the writer and replace the written thought in the position assigned to it by the author of *L'Œuvre?* Why did Zola renounce the task ? Let us, at all events, thank him for drawing up the plan of the battle and being the first to engage in the fight. He failed, not from any baseness of character, but from an error of judgment.

V

The mistake which the great writer made in his life, owing to an inherent defect of his intelligence, he made also in his work; and just as a single weakness was enough to destroy the symmetrical frame of a very noble life, so one single error of judgment was enough to disturb his literary epic, which might, in its breadth and its virile strength, have been one of the most helpful outcomes of the human mind.

Émile Zola's production was one of the most considerable of the last century. That the glory of this powerful novelist is at present under a cloud is due, no doubt, primarily to defects which we will presently consider; partly, also, to a rebound of public opinion, which is always sullenly hostile to those who disappear after having played a large part in life. Chateaubriand, Lamartine, Hugo, Renan, and all those who stirred men's hearts and minds—

all who, as long as they were alive, attracted the crowd
to them by a sort of irresistible magnetism—fell into an
apparent oblivion as soon as their eyes were closed. It
seems as if the crowd, compelled so long to listen to the
echo of the same voice and the turmoil of sentiments
that seethes round any dominating personality, grows
tired of its effort and takes its revenge as soon as the
prestige of the living writer ceases. So Émile Zola is
now passing through the purgatory of a relative obscurity
before he reaches the empyrean of his final glory. How
much of him will survive? That is very difficult to
foresee, in view of the colossal change that is taking place
in literary standards for the last half-century.

I do not know whether the future will preserve the
complete works of recent writers as we have kept those of
earlier masters. I believe that fame in the future will
rather take the form of appreciating the synthetic effort
of great writers, their originality and their creative conceptions, and will not be concerned with the details of
their works. They will survive in the movement they
have given to the guiding ideas of the race rather than
in the perfection of a sonnet or the emotion of a novel.
The great poet will increasingly have to be a great man,
or he will die out entirely. He will have to write masterpieces, not to live for ages, but to contribute to the
advance of humanity. Probably we shall not be read
by our descendants. What does it matter? We shall
have worked for them; and, if we have worked nobly
and strongly, they will remember it. These are inevitable changes which we must contemplate without complaint, just as we accept the laws of evolution. And,
after all, perhaps it is better. The great writer will cease
to belong to history on a small scale—the history of
literature—and pass into the larger history. They will

speak of the future Dantes, Goethes, and Hugos, as we speak about Pericles, Sixtus V., Robespierre, or Napoleon. Poets will not be merely makers of libraries; they will be stages in the human agitation. So much the better.

This prospect which seems to have pleased the serene intelligence of Renan*—though he had a little regret on the artistic side—seems to have terrified the narrower spirit of Zola. He says:

> A graver consequence, and one that has always troubled me, is the continuous effort to which the writer of our time is condemned. We are no longer in the days when a sonnet read in a salon made a writer's reputation and opened the Academy to him. The works of Boileau, La Bruyère, or La Fontaine fill only one or two volumes. . . . Now we have to go on producing unceasingly. *That is terrible*, as it at once raises the question: *What will posterity do in face of this voluminous work?* The memory of man hesitates before such piles of luggage. . . . I have, therefore, always been anxious. We cannot suppose that everything will be kept, yet how will the selection be made? Reflect that the works that have come down to us are all short in comparison with ours. If it is true that every writer has only one book in him, we are doing *something that compromises our own glory* in our infinite repetitions of this book, under the lash of new needs. There, in my opinion, is the only disturbing consequence of the actual state of things. Nor can we ever judge the future by the past. Balzac will survive under very different conditions from Boileau.

In the last two sentences Zola seems to perceive and accept the situation. But it troubles him. The man of letters was always breaking out in him.

Yes, "Balzac will survive under very different conditions from Boileau," and Zola under different conditions from La Bruyère. Will people read *L'Assommoir, Nana, Germinal, L'Œuvre*, or *Les Évangiles?* I do not know. I do not think so. Apart from the indifference which posterity will increasingly feel for works of the past, Zola's works in particular are too much impregnated

* See Note 9 (at end of volume).

with the atmosphere of a period to survive long. Renan,
of the ironic smile, saw the oblivion to which realistic
works were inevitably doomed:

> The future will, perhaps, not have much time to read us. It
> will be too much taken up with itself to pay attention to us.
> *I fear that the self-sacrifice of our realist writers, who say that their*
> *only purpose is to provide documents from which future ages may*
> *know us, will be poorly rewarded.*

It is probable, nay it is certain, that all the works of
men of letters of the naturalist school, will be dead a few
generations from now, if they are not already dead.*
But Zola will survive, because his work is far higher
than that of his imitators and pupils. Even when he is
no longer read page by page, he will survive in fame;
and what remains of him will be great. He will survive
by his example of splendid energy, untiring will, and
proud dignity, in spite of the weaknesses I noticed. These
are virtues of the man. We find them in his work, and
they constitute its greatness.

But beyond these qualities of vigour, power, and epic
breadth in his work, of which others have spoken repeatedly, it has one merit which surpasses all the others
and confers upon it a splendour that is, perhaps, unique
amongst the works of the nineteenth century, if not of
the whole of French literature. It is *one:* it is organic.

VI

This merit we cannot exaggerate. It is the best title
to fame that Zola will retain, and by which he will win
posterity. At present we do not see the full beauty of
this admirable enterprise, because we are too close to the
man who ventured upon it, because the poorer writers

* See Note 10 (at end of volume).

of our time still linger in academic games, or in the purely industrial aspects of work that has no unity. But when a few strong spirits have swept out of literature all these follies of the salon and business requirements of the bookshop, when prouder and nobler generations have arisen to understand the luminous mission of the writer, I doubt not that the architectural conception of the *Rougon-Macquart* will seem an heroic and robust example of what the deliberate work of a master mind ought to be.

Yes, let us say it firmly, because for our children it will be an indisputable truth: a literary work must, like all human work, aim at unity. That is a law against which the mediocre rebel, and will continue to rebel, but the strong will accept it as they accept the harmonious order of the universe. Why should it be different for poetic creations than for any others ? Does a genius in science, philosophy or politics scatter itself ? Do the discoverers of new forces, the inventors of systems, the founders of empires, spend themselves in detached and successive efforts ? Do you see a Newton, a Plato, a Spinoza, a Descartes, a Richelieu, a Peter the Great, try twenty different unconnected works ?

It must be the same with the poet. In earlier centuries, when literature was only a pastime of men of letters, it was possible for writers to attain fame by disconnected fragments; but it will not be the same in the formidable movement of the new world. We have to give up more and more the idea of dominating and surviving by talent alone. In the world-conflict of ideas and races, every work will perish that has not a universal influence. There will be nothing left of these isolated works, written on the casual spur of inspiration, fancy, caprice, or fashion; nothing of the volumes whose author skips from subject to subject, which have nothing in common but the author's

signature. Posterity, which will not have much leisure
to read us, will reject everything that was merely intended
to fill up the time.   There will be left only those who have
embodied one powerful guiding idea in a synthetic work.
Even if the work is no longer read, the dominant idea
will easily survive in the influence it has had and in its
contribution to history.

Zola was the first to understand, formulate, and dis-
charge this splendid function of the writer.   It is true
that Balzac had already written his *Human Comedy*.
But the synthesis of this work was more or less unconscious
on the part of the author of *Lost Illusions*.   He did not
see the link between his works until afterwards.   He
reached the synthesis by the impulse of his genius rather
than by an effort of will.   Moreover, many of his works
are casual, and have no connection with the main theme.
We need not add that, conscious or unconscious, deliberate
or spontaneous, the *Human Comedy* is, on account of its
architectural spaciousness and the general idea which
inspires it, Balzac's chief title to glory.   It will not be
forgotten even when it is no longer read.

Well, Zola will have the same glory.   He will have, in
addition, the admiration of posterity for the clearness
with which his genius conceived the organism of his
work from the start, the tenacity with which he realised
it, the power he brought to the task.

I can quote nothing more moving in this respect than
two fragments of *L'Œuvre*, in which the novelist Sandoz,
who reflects Zola himself, explains to his friend Claude
the vague idea of the great work of which he is dreaming
and then the broad plan of the work he has already
begun.   At the beginning of his career Sandoz says:

How fine it would be to give one's entire life to a work in which
one would try to put things and beasts and men—the whole

immense vault! Not in the style of manuals of philosophy, according to the silly hierarchy in which our pride finds comfort, but in the full flow of universal life: a world in which we are a mere accident, in which the passing dog, even the pebble on the path, completes and explains us: the great whole, without high or low, without clean or dirty, such as it lives. . . . Oh, if I knew, if I knew, what a series of books I would throw at the crowd's head !

A few years later the same Sandoz—Zola all the time— has discovered the generating idea of the synthesis he sought, and he gets to work with a cry of enthusiasm:

Well, I have found what I wanted. Oh, nothing big—just a little corner, enough for a human life, even when one's ambition is too large. . . . I am going to take a family and study its members one by one—whence they come, whither they are going, how they react upon each other. A bit of humanity apart, the way in which men act and behave. On the other hand, I will put my characters in a particular historical period, which will give me the environment and conditions—a bit of history. . . . Do you see ? A series of books—fifteen, twenty books. Episodes that will hang together, while each has its own sphere. A series of novels that will build a house for me in my old age—if they don't crush me. . . .

Dear earth, who art our common mother, the one source of life, take me ! Thou, the eternal, the immortal, in whom is the soul of the world, the sap that flows even in stones and makes the trees our great motionless brothers ! Yes, I want to lose myself in thee. It is thee I feel, underneath my limbs, clasping and inflaming me. Thou alone shalt be the primary force of my work, the means and the end, the immense vault under which all things are animated by the life of all beings.

The man who wrote this—and his whole work was an impressive commentary on it—was quickened by one of the most generous geniuses that ever whispered in human brain. It is the man who, in the struggles of *Une Campagne*, discovered this lofty formula: "My feeling is that the triumph of a single idea demands the life of a man." Let us do him the justice he deserves. Zola is a splendid writer in his effort to attain a synthesis and the courageous consciousness he had of that effort.

VII

How is it then that, if I so much admire him and acknowledge the virtues of his character and the energy of his creative genius, I put him amongst the "bad masters"? It is because in these essays I take no notice of the disinterested but childish passions, the empty and unjust quarrels, of literary schools. I have no prejudice for or against the writers with whom I deal. I belong to no school and no group. What I have said about Zola proves my impartiality, I venture to think, or, at all events, my attempt to be impartial. From me you will get neither prejudice against the man nor hatred of his ideas in the task, which I now approach, of showing what initial fault there was in Zola's conception of his work that made him, in spite of his generous and devoted labour, have a certain amount of evil influence and create an unfortunate current in the mind of his readers.

The great misfortune of Émile Zola was that his intelligence was not equal to his genius and his character. Let us have the courage to say it—he was not "intelligent." As a matter of fact, there is nothing so rare as real intelligence. The word "intelligence," which is used so loosely in daily life, and applied indifferently to ingenious lads, successful drapers, or sagacious reporters, means, in its literal and full sense, one of the finest and most comprehensive powers of the human mind. *Intelligere*, to understand, to choose, to judge, is the marvellous gift which certain minds have of embracing the whole race in all the ceaseless movement of its passions, its virtues, its desires, and its works. It is the power of judging individuals and peoples with serenity, to put everything in its proper place, and to be surprised at no accident. How few men have ever had this marvellous faculty! How few have even approached it ! Great geniuses—men with temperament, originality, and creative force—have lacked intelligence; great characters have been wholly without it. There have really been very few men of complete intelligence in history, as were, in modern times, Rabelais, Goethe, and Renan. Ah! if Zola had had the intelligence of Renan, or Renan the character of Zola! But we will not waste time in useless regrets. We have to take men as they are, and works as they are, and derive whatever lesson we can from good and evil.

Zola was wanting in breadth of mind. One has only to read his critical works to realise this. I have already said how we must admire the intrepidity of his literary campaigns, the splendour of his single-handed fights against everybody. But, while these collections of articles and essays reveal a fine and proud character, a vigorous will, an ardent passion for truth, and sometimes a perception as swift as lightning, let us acknowledge that they show some narrowness of mind, violent prejudice, an obstinate unwillingness to admit what the author does not understand or does not like.

These were, I shall be told, inevitable defects in the head of a school. I do not admit it. Injustice and partiality are never necessary; moreover, it is never necessary to be the head of a school. It is a puerility of the salon or the café. The Dantes and Goethes did not exert themselves to marshal and lead flocks of mediocre followers. They flung into the world the finest and broadest work they could, and let the message work. But let us pass on. Head of a school or no, it is certain that Zola had a prejudiced and narrow mind. Now this is precisely the contrary of intelligence. The verdicts which he passes on the great writers of former times in the course of his controversies make one smile sometimes.

Vergil, Plato, Dante, Corneille, Racine—all the great
poets he regards as " rhetoricians." He gives the title
" rhetorician " to everybody who was not of the naturalist
school. Very curious, in this respect, is the verdict Zola
passes on Renan in his *Lettre à la jeunesse :* " He was not
a believer; but he was not a scholar." And a little later
Zola naïvely says: " We scholars . . ."

No doubt Zola's genius was not based upon that solid
classical culture without which even the strongest brain
will fail to embrace the whole of humanity. It is by no
caprice of language that we give the name of " Human-
ists " to those who were reared on the marrow of humane
letters. Without this general knowledge, slowly and
imperceptibly assimilated during childhood, which is the
solid scaffolding of the mind, even the most gifted man
cannot rise high above his age; if his genius carries him
up, he becomes dizzy, as if he had no serene standpoint
from which to contemplate the agitation of the world.

It is clear that Zola had not the sense of antiquity,
nor even, to any extent, the sense of history. Lacking
elevation of prospect, he greatly exaggerated the importance of his age; which is a common mistake of
imperfectly developed intelligences. Zola was terrified
by the formidable movement of his age, and he felt the
slightest reactions. We have already seen how his lack
of serenity marred his career. It had a very bad influence
on his work. His character, in spite of everything, may
be seen at a distance in all its beauty; his work remains
confused.

VIII

In the first place, in spite of the force of the conception,
the life which animates it, and the genius which sustains
it, his work lacks greatness. So much labour, so much

inspiration—for what ? To tell the story of a neurotic family of the Second Empire ! However, let the scene of it pass. The poet has a right to place his world where he pleases—provided it is the world. The events which fill the *Iliad* lasted only a few days. Those with which the *Odyssey* deals occupied only a few years. The whole cycle of the two Homeric poems falls within less than twenty years, or less than the *Rougon-Macquart*. But from Nestor to Eumæus, from Achilles to Ulysses, from Agamemnon to Alcinous, from Hector to Telemachus, from Helena to Penelope, from Andromache to Nausicaa, from Calchas to Demodocus, from Thersites to Eurimache, what a complete gamut of the passions, the heroisms, the virtues, and the base vices ! From the King of kings to the drunken sailor everything is alive and stirring, everything shares the action; and the large and varied choir of the crowds rumbles unceasingly round the actions of the characters, good and bad. Even the horses neigh in the battle, and the dogs die of tenderness. Within those twenty years the whole of life passes. And three thousand years later the work seems to us fresher than a story published to-day.

Zola was therefore quite at liberty to put the whole immense world in the quarter of a century of the *Rougon-Macquart*. What does the environment or the period matter ? Man is the same always and everywhere. In city attics and in the palaces of kings, under the silk hat or the steel helmet, it is the same souls that quiver, the same passions that ferment, the same vices that grow, the same straining toward the azure. In Zola's time as well as in Homer's time there were Helenas and Penelopes, Thersites and Achilles, Ulysses and Menelaus, perfidious Circes and generous Eumæi—there was a whole race. Did Zola see it ? Did he refashion it ?

Did he give it life ? I appeal to those who still have his
work in mind. His world is really only a small corner
of the world. It is not a picture of the whole man; it is a
picture of ephemeral and superficial manners. It is the
accident of a period.

If he had at least made a synthesis of the period!
He did not; he depicted only its vices and weaknesses.
Unbalanced men, scoundrels, thieves, prostitutes,
drunkards, stupid dreamers, unhealthy peasants, degraded
workers, unclean bourgeois, cowardly soldiers, avaricious
ministers, feeble artists, hysterical priests—all this is
offered to us as a mirror of human nature. Not a single
great man, not an elect soul, not a noble and strong
individuality, not a hero—that is supposed to be the
measure of our time. No joy, no triumphant effort, not
a single healthy development—this is a picture of our
life. We are promised a world, and we get a hospital.
Surely this is incredible ignorance or incredible perversity !

No. The man who accomplished this work was neither
ignorant nor perverse. He was a man of energy and
conscience: a fine man. He led a noble life, and had the
most generous intentions. He sought the truth devotedly;
he thought that he had found it, and that he spoke it.
He was mistaken, but mistaken in good faith. And his
mistake was all the more mischievous on account of the
power of his genius. We know how we must admire
his design of a synthesis. But this synthesis itself,
by the strength it gives to Zola's work, makes his
influence all the more terrible; for it was false from the
start.

Zola's mistake, the defect of his intelligence, betrays
itself in the fundamental principle of his work. In sum,
the principle is:

To apply to the study of man and society the experimental and documented method of the physical, chemical, and natural sciences.

He makes Claude Bernard responsible for the theory of naturalist literature, which he constantly calls "scientific." According to Zola, everything that is mere hypothesis, not verified by observation and experience, must be rejected. The writer must paint and refashion only what he has himself observed, or learned from documents which he has controlled. If he does this, he creates a useful, fruitful, enduring work, like the chemist. Further, he is a great moralist:

We seek the causes of social evil. We dissect classes and individuals in order to elucidate the aberrations of society and man. This compels us often to work on abnormal subjects, to go down into the midst of man's miseries and follies. But we give the necessary documents so that, besides knowing them, we may be masters of the good and the evil. That is what we have, in all sincerity, seen, observed, and explained. Now it is for our legislators to bring out and develop the good, to struggle against and uproot the evil. *Hence no work could have a greater moral influence than ours*, because the law must be based upon it·

And elsewhere, in a concise formula, he says:

The only great and moral works are works of truth.

Clearly, Zola's intention was most praiseworthy. His sincerity is beyond question. He has a system, and it seems, at first sight, solid and good: the search for truth by experience. In reality, it is absurd.

Yes, it is absurd to compare the study of man with the study of nature. When the chemist analyses natural forces, all the elements seem to him to have the same intensity, whether they be useful or harmful, creative or destructive. In humanity, on the other hand, there is an imponderable and incommensurable element, and this shows itself sometimes very plainly, and at other times is hidden under the most invisible folds: it is the soul.

The more vile and corrupt it is, the easier it is to study.
The nobler and purer it is, the less it is seen. Observation
alone is an illusion. Have you never noticed that all the
famous observers are misanthropic and discouraging?
Take La Bruyère, La Rochefoucauld, Molière, or La
Fontaine. They were observers of genius; and their
work is sad and false, because in it mankind seems to
be thoroughly bad. Whenever some noble person, an
Alcestis, does appear, he is marred by a ridiculous exterior.
It is because observation only seizes vice, perversity,
baseness; for evil displays itself, and goodness hides.

Go into a drawing-room or a public meeting. All that
is odious in it will strike you at once, in spite of any
attempt at hypocrisy. You immediately recognise the
debauchee, the slave of passion or vanity, the gambler,
the fool. They reveal themselves to your eyes. But if
there is any person of great virtue present, I defy you to
find him; because if he let himself be seen, he would lose
the quality of his virtue, which is a proud reserve. It is
the same in the street. There is the prostitute, the
drunkard, or the idler—you have only to pass by them
to recognise them. But here is a mother who goes on her
way, alone, in silence and sorrow, to take some painful
step or do something humiliating to save an unhappy
child. How will you guess that? Here is a man hurrying
along, looking distracted, walking as if he were an auto-
maton. He is going to help a friend somewhere, to
resign himself to some sacrifice, complete a masterpiece,
perhaps. What can you see of all that? Nothing.
The most sagacious observer will prove blind. And if
one were to carry this experience through all the theatres
of the human comedy, one would hear everywhere the
echoes of folly and vice and vanity; but one would know
nothing about virtue, for it is isolated and silent.

IX

That is why these supposed observers have depicted only the moral uglinesses of the world. Their works never contain a hero. In Zola's case the defect is pushed to extremes, because he makes a narrow system of observation and experiment, and is, as is known, blindly obstinate in it.

There is no hero in the *Rougon-Macquart*, no superior being, no saint, no genius. Fine natures of this kind do not exist for Zola. He has not seen them. They have not come under the lens of his experience, so they are inventions of poets. The " scholar " must reject them. These miserable systems ! Why must even genius fall into such absurdities ?

What, there are no great souls ? No sublime virtue ? No heroes ? And you call that the truth ! Look beyond the little field to which you have confined your short-sighted eyes. Look into the history of the earth. The hero an invention of the poet ? Beyond question the moment a Plato or a Dante, a Marcus Aurelius or a Vincent de Paul, a Leonidas, a Bayard, a La Tour d'Auvergne—to quote only a few names—came into existence, the hero existed. But nothing is lost in humanity, any more than in nature. Therefore, as the hero has existed, he still exists, and always will exist. It is your business to seek him, to find him, to make him live in your world: otherwise your world is incomplete, false. Yes, look for the hero. He does not, of course, now wear the armour of Achilles or the toga of Brutus. He is not necessarily ornamental and romantic. He has not a revolution or a battle-field for his theatre. He is wherever the struggle for life brings out lofty souls and vile souls. He is in the attic, in the cottage, in the vessel that goes down at sea. Let the occasion arise, and his heroism will shine upon the eyes of the world. Very often he dies without the world knowing anything about him. I have myself known splendid heroes who sleep, unknown, in obscure cemeteries. Did Zola never know any? Were there none in his days? None in his own world? Strange blindness! He need only have looked at himself in a mirror, for he had the soul of a hero. Yet as an author he dared not put in his work the hero that he was, and that others of his world were. That is his apostleship of truth! He did not *dare*—that is precisely his fault. Brave man as he was, he had a strange cowardice. He was afraid of his own theories. Free man as he was, he submitted to the saddest slavery. He was a prisoner of his own system. A militant naturalist, he was afraid of seeming an idealist.

Idealist! The ideal! The words made him lose his head. He rushed upon them furiously, like a mad bull upon the red *muleta*. He stubbornly refused to see the meaning of them. For him ideals were the blue dreams of fairy tales, the azure dreams of idyllic poets. Never was a real genius made so stupid by obstinately clinging to a preconceived theory. He did not see that the ideal was just what he was trying to realise: a noble and sustained effort to do something great. From fear of appearing an idealist, the brave knight *did not dare be* himself. Real fact as he was, he *did not dare* open out his wings toward the sky.

Did not dare? Well, he dared; but it was too late. Zola's last works are a flagrant contradiction of the whole teaching of the *Rougon-Macquart*. Suddenly, under the influence of a salutary crisis, his soul opened, his mind was enlarged, the bonds he had forged broke and fell away. Beyond superficial and transitory phenomena the new Zola dimly perceives life, real life, the life that the eyes of the body are not sharp enough to see, but for which poets seem to have eyes in their genius. He realises the straining of the race toward the light. He feels the nobleness of souls and the beauty of lofty lives. He sees heroes at last; and he proves that in the study of complex and mysterious man one must have intuition as well as experience. One must be a *seer* as well as an observer.

Unhappily, it was too late. His strong and industrious brain, accustomed to different ideas, seemed to refuse entrance to this new world. One would almost say that the wheels of the powerful machine were worn too far to permit so complete a change. *Les Évangiles*, in spite of the fervent idea that animates it, is a vague and indecisive work; and *L'Assommoir* and *Nana* had been so strong and definite. So the splendid and sorrowful Icarus, opening his tardy wings, fell, vanquished, in his last heroic effort.

Thus of the whole of Zola's work there remains only the *Rougon-Macquart*, that immense and troubled world, with its hospital exhalations spreading an odour of disease and despair, giving out an unwholesome poison, a demoralising pessimism. That is how, through an error of intelligence, Zola, the noble and manly genius, produced a nocturnal and enfeebling work. In expelling from his world the ideal that he bore in his own heart, he was like a painter who, to portray more accurately the forms and movements of the earth, should want to leave out the vivifying splendour of the sun.

EPILOGUE

THE RENAISSANCE OF THE CLASSICAL
SPIRIT

(FRÉDÉRIC MISTRAL)

I wish, as the health-giving fragrance I cull,
That thy breast with strong thoughts could for ever be full,
And that, rhythmic'ly flowing, thy Christian blood
Could resemble the old-time metrical flood.

BAUDELAIRE: *The Sick Muse* (Scott).

EPILOGUE

THE RENAISSANCE OF THE CLASSICAL SPIRIT

THE presentation of the *Iphigénie* of Jean Moréas in the ancient theatre at Orange is for the moment [1903] a genuine literary event. The most important organs of French opinion informed us that the public wept with emotion on hearing the tragic lines of the poet. Others reproduced whole pages of the manuscript. Some explained the work, and gave an account of Jean Moréas; while others, hardly recovered from their astonishment, were sparing in their praise, though they acknowledged the reality of the success. Everybody, in Paris and the provinces, kept repeating that there really is something new in the intellectual atmosphere of France.

There is, in fact, in the echoes which reach us from Orange something more than the usual fuss made about a new work that succeeds in the theatre. In this success, which was expected and desired by the public, especially by the young men, there is an indication of a general stirring of ideas, a striking manifestation of an awakening which literary men had foreseen, a symptom of a classical renaissance.

If there are any unknown friends who have followed the preceding essays with interest, they will understand the special pleasure with which I greet this new dawn. But doubtless it will be thought by many that my eagerness to see this dawn has prompted me to mistake some light that appears on the horizon for a moment for the rise

of a new sun. I am therefore going to prove the reality
of this renaissance by giving broader indications. Indeed,
the discussion of the matter itself assures me that I am
not alone in my expectation and my hope.

I

And, first, what *is* this classical " spirit " which we
declare to be reawakening ? Few words have been more
disturbed in their meaning, more misunderstood, in
literary discussion than the word " classical." Yet it has
such a substantial meaning, it expresses so well one of the
essential ideas of art, that, in spite of all the abuse, it
always comes back. It is the inevitable, the only
intelligible, word to use when we want to express the idea
or group of ideas for which it stands.

Say to a man who has any tincture of letters, " This
is a classical work," or " This is classic beauty," or " That
is a classic idea." He will at once know what you mean,
if not in the finer shades, at all events in a general way.
Aulus Gellius used the phrase *classicus auctor* to denote
an absolutely perfect author—one of the first rank, one
in whom everything worked for perfection and was bound
to endure. That is the meaning which, in spite of all
distortions, the word " classical " still has in our own
time. Let us see, then, what the essential qualities are
which have to be found in conjunction to give the enduring,
finished, splendid beauty that the word implies.

First, there is moral wholesomeness. " I call classical
all that is wholesome," said Goethe, " and romantic all
that is sickly." All things considered, there is nothing to
alter in this aphorism. Is it complete ? That we shall
see presently. In any case, it gives in a neat formula the
very essence of the classical spirit.

Let us take the great periods of human history which all historians agree to call "classical." They were culminating points at which all forms of human thought, embodied in solidly conceived and harmoniously executed works of art, met together and co-operated in forming a combination of energy, order, and beauty. All the vanities of exaggerated individualism, all the deficiencies of rebellious passion, all the fantasies of personal and futile taste, all the follies of feminine caprice—all these putrefactions of morbid civilisations were naturally excluded from the clear and strong life of the time, just as the germs of dank and dark places are exterminated by the sun's rays.

Let us study these classical ages, and we shall see what is characteristic of them—collective strength. Individuals and groups harmonise and complete each other like the various parts of an architectural masterpiece. We have Sophocles together with Pheidias and Mnesicles, Thucydides with Xenophon, Plato with Aristotle, Titus Livius joining with Vergil in chanting the glory of ancient Rome, Petrarch completing Dante, the Spain of Lope de Vega, Calderon, and Cervantes, the England of Shakespeare and Bacon, the Germany of Goethe, Schiller, Lessing, and Herder; and, whatever towering height may be reached by the great geniuses of these periods, the personality of each disappears in the broad wealth of a national or universal art. And this law is most strikingly seen in the development of the two great classical periods, the Italy of the Renaissance and the France of Louis XIV. Here the glory of the great artists and writers blends, in a sense, with all contemporary glories, and such a thing as an isolated genius is unthinkable. Michael Angelo, Leonardo, Bramante, Raphael, Titian, and Veronese cannot be understood apart from each other. Corneille,

Descartes, Pascal, Racine, Bossuet, Molière, La Fontaine, and La Bruyère, are linked together, and complete each other, in a continuous order. All of them take part in a sort of ideal movement which is their age. One no more thinks of separating them than one would think of separating the columns of the Parthenon or the frescoes of the Sistine Chapel.

Hence there is a fine healthiness in their work, a great vigour in the development of their minds. All these geniuses are clear, radiant, and beautiful; and each develops with perfect ease and smoothness, as the branches of a strong, well-planted tree develop. Flowers and fruit appear in due season, not interfering with each other's growth.

In these classic ages you look in vain for these miserable groans of vague sadness, of amorous melancholy, of pain, finding pleasure in themselves and in all the individual miseries collected in romantic poetry. The great and strong creators let us see nothing of their personal tears. Like all others, they have their " great sorrows," but by means of these sorrows, which their will has mastered, they have distilled out of their hearts the deep and tranquil pity which has given birth to all works that ennoble the race.

This, then, is the first virtue required in a classical work—moral health, strength. But is this enough? No, for we know plenty of sound and strong works which we cannot call classical. There must also be absolute perfection of taste, perfect balance of reason and imagination, complete freedom from exaggeration; in a word, a " measure," which gives to creations of man's mind the harmony and regularity of the eternal laws.

We do not find this ideal, ordered, serene perfection in the history of the cities and works constructed by man before the birth of Greece. India knew it not, nor did Egypt: much less heavy and magnificent Asia. In fact, therefore, the classic spirit goes back to that golden age of the mind which we call Hellenism. Its first apostle was Orpheus, or, if you like, the sum of doctrines and symbols which has been personified in his name. The classic spirit was born when Orpheus gave supremacy to the solar spirit over all others, when he expelled from his cult all dark, nocturnal influences and replaced them by light, when he repelled the Bacchantes, the daughters of disturbance, and loved only Eurydice, the incarnation of clearness.

This classical or solar spirit inspires those whom it animates with an unfailing love of struggle and life on the one hand, and, on the other, with resignation to the inevitable laws of destiny. By an adjustment of these apparently contradictory ideas it brings about order in the mind. If the love of struggle—the " strength " of which we have already spoken—is not tempered by resignation to the immutable laws of the world, it issues in rebellion against those laws, in a state of anger and passion, the lyrical disorder which we call " romantic." On the other hand, if resignation to inevitable laws be not vivified by a love of life and desire to struggle, it ends in the annihilation of Oriental fatalism. Between the Nirvana of the East and the unrestrained fury of the Celtic warriors, who shot their arrows at the sky, Greece discovered this supreme harmony; and the word " Hellenism " alone expresses the whole beauty of it.

Finally, the classical spirit gives those whose mind it illumines the power of seeing things always in a perfectly sharp perspective, enabling them to ignore every useless and secondary aspect and to fix the attention only on the essential and properly ordered lines.

That is why strength and health alone are not enough for a classical work. It must, above all, imply serenity of life and perfection of art. It gives birth to Minerva, and builds the Parthenon. The two are inseparable.

This solar spirit, the spirit of Orpheus, survived in its entirety in Greece. It passed to Italy, where it animated the work of Vergil. It was preserved, apart, through all the torments of the Middle Ages. It awoke Dante, Petrarch, and the whole of the Renaissance. In the fulness of time it came to France, where it found in the smiling bravery of the race and the pleasant mildness of the climate the most favourable soil for producing the flowers of which it bore the germs.

Well, this luminous Hellenism, which seemed to have disappeared from French work, is in honour once more: like those kindly aged relatives whom one abandons in hours of disorder, and to whom, as natural guides, one returns when one seems to be on the brink of calamity.

II

But is not this case of Moréas an exception, an accident, in contemporary literary history ? By his very origin, his direct Athenian descent, was not the author of *Eriphyle*, *Stances*, and *Iphigénie* brought by a personal and exceptional predilection, quite apart from any movement in his environment, to restore the cult of purely classical art in France ? If that is so, the supposed classical renaissance is merely a literary curiosity, only calculated to interest a few men of letters and devotees of art, of no importance in the history of our time. For in literary history, just as in social and political history, what is accidental does not exist. Only that which bears upon the general movement of ideas and life deserves to hold the attention of the public.

One of two things, therefore. Either the appearance of works of a classical tendency, like *Stances* and *Iphigénie*, is no more than an anachronistic accident, or the success of these works corresponds with some expectation or need of the soul of France. In the first case the works are not important enough for us to deal with them, and Jean Moréas merely takes his place in an anthology. But if the second alternative is true, the classical renaissance indicated by the works which the public has just applauded is not an isolated fact, of chance origin, and it is worth while seeking the reasons for this renaissance in the history of the last century. That is why, in the interest of the cause itself, as well as for the credit of the new writers who are attempting to give France once more a strong and lofty classical literature, it is important to find whence they come, so that one may judge how far they are likely to go.

In reality, the classical spirit, with all the light, serenity, strength, lightness of spirit, and inspiration which it involves, was restored in France half a century ago. And the man whose sunny genius gave us once more the pure light of Hellenism is to-day in the full radiance of his glory and the full vigour of his influence: Frédéric Mistral. It was Mistral who brought about the classical renaissance in France, and it is fitting to express to-day the gratitude which French literature owes him.

I say advisedly " French literature," and I ought to add " the French language," however strange these phrases may at first seem to superficial minds. They will be astonished to hear that the French language and literature can owe anything to a man who seems to have lived in revolt against them, even in hostility to them: to a poet who deliberately tried to create a literature alongside of, even rival to, our national literature, and to bring back to life beside our great language an idiom that had fallen out of use.

Yet it is unquestionably true, and it is enough to study impartially the work and life of Mistral to realise the whole of the inspiration they have given to a new generation of French writers. Destiny seems, at first sight, to have impenetrable secrets, and they seem, when we discover them, to be due to some sort of super-human irony. Perhaps Mistral himself was rather surprised at the results of his work upon us. If he was, his surprise would not last long, for he is the exact opposite of an unconscious genius. He sees with marvellous clearness the effect which his writings and conduct may have in the future.

We have to agree with him. The Provençal renaissance brought about by Mistral is responsible for the renaissance of the pure French spirit; which proves that no effort is ever wasted. No poet in the whole history of letters was more completely, more purely, more naturally saturated with the Hellenic spirit—more *classical*, in a word—than Mistral. He belongs to the same great, luminous family as Homer, Plato, Vergil, Dante, Petrarch, and Racine. Of all his intellectual ancestors the one he approaches most nearly in spirit and form is Vergil. It seems as if the same breath, purified by the snow of the Alps, vivified by the breezes of the Mediterranean, animated the mind of the two poets, born almost in the same latitude: the one on the banks of a tributary of the Po, the other on a tributary of the Rhone. These two Gallo-Romans, one of Cisalpine, and one of Transalpine Gaul, both nourished by the purest Hellenic sap, displayed in their twin styles the fairest and brightest flowers of human poetry.

Mistral is, like Vergil, irreproachable in his choice of words, in the clearness and simplicity of his figures of speech, and in the crystalline limpidity of his language, so transparent that at first it seems to have no depth, yet so full of meaning that, after long consideration, one hardly sees the bottom of it. And what measure, what tact, what truth in his magnificent idyllic pictures! What sustained harmony! What faultless purity! In French letters only Racine and Fénelon have this marvellous limpidity; but the Provençal tongue, like the Latin, has, in addition, some taste of the sun that is lacking in our less coloured and less concrete tongue.

III

Such, during fifty years, without faltering, has the fine classic poet of *Mireille* and *Calendal* developed. But he has not only restored to us the clear speech and luminous visions of the Helleno-Roman civilisation. He is also an incarnation of the balanced wisdom, the free boldness, and the robust serenity of imperishable Hellenism. He is wholly and entirely classical, in spirit as well as form.

Mistral had the noblest ideal of the poet which it is possible to have. He has been the shepherd of peoples, the moral guide of the generations in which he lived, the teacher of energy to future generations. Never perhaps had the *os magna sonaturum* of Horace a more striking application. He sang only of beautiful things, he extolled only fine sentiments, and he evoked only great thoughts, because he himself, naturally, from inborn nobleness, could attempt nothing that was not great. He is unquestionably of that elect body which Vergil makes Æneas meet in the woods of his Elysian fields:

Quique pii vates et Phœbo digna locuti.

Listen, for instance, to this splendid appeal, worthy of Vergil or Dante, with which Mistral begins his *Calendal :*

Soul of my country—thou who dost shine in all its story and its tongue—when the barons of Picardy, of Germany, and of Burgundy—swarmed round Toulouse and Beaucaire—thou who didst fire on every side—against the black riders—the men of Marseilles and the sons of Avignon.

By these great memories of the past—thou who dost save and hope—thou who, in our youth, still warmer and more generous —in spite of death and the digger, dost bring back the blood of our fathers—thou, inspirer of the sweet troubadours—and like the *mistral* dost later make the voice of Mirabeau roar.

For the seas of the ages—and their storms and their horrors— in vain mix the nations and their frontiers efface ; our mother-earth, nature, still feeds her sons—with the same milk; her hard breast still gives its fine oil to the olive.

Soul ever rising anew,—joyous and proud and alive—who dost neigh in the noise of the Rhone and its wind;—soul of the woods full of harmony—and of the sunny bays—pious soul of my country—I call upon thee, incarnate thyself in my Provençal verse !

Do not these accents of pride and strength take us far away from the lamentable effusions of sickly love or sterile dream and all the individualist follies which Romanticism extolled in the last century ? And what poet has better expressed the great ideal of classic poetry than the man whose whole poetic art is summed up in these two simple and sublime verses of his *Chant de la coupe ?*

Pour out the poet's wine,
    Singing of man and God,
For 'tis the food divine
    That lifts the human clod.

Grant us the power to know
    Things good and true and brave,
And every joy bestow
    That laughs e'en at the grave.

Compare this conception of the poet with, for instance, the following from Musset:

> Madder than fair Ophelia with rosemary crowned,
> Sillier than page who for love of fairy has swooned,
> Played the tambourine on his shattered headgear.

Or with this of Verlaine:

> The fine shade ! The fine shade !
> 'Tis that alone marries
> The dream to the dream, and the flute to the horn.

Passing from pure poetry to history we find that Mistral, both in his lyric and his epic poems, displays, whenever he conjures up the harmonious evolution of his beautiful country, the perfect balance of imagination and reason, the blend of wisdom and energy, which are the essence of the classical spirit. It is he who (in his *Ode aux poètes catalans*) wrote these two lines:

> For now it is plain, now at last do we know,
> That in the order divine all things work for good.

To this lofty ideal of the poet as the shepherd of nations, Mistral was faithful all his life, without the least lapse, without any Utopia, in virtue of the perfect balance of his genius. That is why his beautiful work, the reflection of his beautiful life, was not merely a matter of literature; it was a matter of conduct. He was not flute-player: he was a torch-bearer. At the end of the nineteenth century and the beginning of the twentieth this villager of Maillane dared to recall the solar mission of the poet, the descendant of Orpheus, the guide of the multitude, and of Amphion, the builder of cities.

But Mistral did more than express the mission of the poet in his fine verses. He realised it. Every poem of his is a fruitful act. Just as Vergil made the *Æneid* the guiding work of Roman thought, as Dante brought on the reawakening of Italy by his *Divine Comedy*, so Mistral, in his *Mireille*, his *Calendal*, and his *Îles d'or*, brought about the renaissance of the Provençal race; then, by repercussion, that of the provinces of France; and finally, as a natural consequence, the reawakening of the classical spirit in the whole of France.

IV

It was impossible for such a man to live anywhere on French soil without the radiation from his work gradually stimulating the generation that grew up around him. What! In the height of a period of naturalism and exaggerated Romanticism, at a time when at Paris all the morbidities of the dream and all the ugliness of brutal realism formed the substance of the literature that was in vogue, in this age of unquestioned decadence, there was a rival of Vergil and Dante in Provence, and a genius of this character could be without influence on France itself? That would be to deny the most essential laws of intellectual development.

As regards the French language, in the first place, we may say that it owes to Mistral as much as the Provençal tongue does. After the invasion of disturbed ideas and disorderly styles which Romanticism had let into our literature by opening wide our doors to the barbarism of the north, we needed purification from the Mediterranean; we needed the bracing tonic of the Græco-Roman sun. France, let us not forget, belongs to the Latin family, and, if it is not to renounce its own genius, it must preserve entire the inheritance it has received from Greece. The *langue d'oïl* and the *langue d'oc* were twin births from the soil which the Gallo-Roman civilisation had fertilised.

The Renaissance of the Classical Spirit

From the eleventh century, the golden age in Occitania, to the seventeenth century, the golden age in the Île de France, through Thibault de Champagne, Froissart, Commines, Charles d'Orléans, Villon, Ronsard, Rabelais, and Montaigne, the *langue d'oc* and *langue d'oïl* had so mingled their sap, like two robust plants closely connected, that they had produced a single fruit: the fine classical style of the seventeenth century.

But a day came when this fruit seemed to rot on the parched branches, and in recent times one would have thought that it was all over with the fresh vegetation of France. Our language and style had, as it were, lost their race, and parasitic growths fastened upon the old tree of France, strangling it down to its very roots. Then came Mistral with his fertilising stream, issuing from the living wells of the *Æneid* and the *Odyssey*, and at one and the same time he restored life to the southern olive and the northern oak, which seemed about to perish.

Sustained by his sunny and limpid work, the newcomers in literature, especially those who had been fortunate enough to have been born in the lands glorified by Mistral, cherished a new regard for clear and harmonious form, on the one hand, and, on the other, a love of general ideas and noble and uplifting conceptions. In short, owing to the paramount influence of the author of *Mireille*—an influence that penetrated slowly, but with the calm sureness of a sun rising upon the horizon—all the young men of the new generation felt that they were impregnated with the classical spirit. Even those who did not know Mistral, who had never read him, felt on their foreheads, without knowing or wishing it, the purifying wind that came, by the southern roads, from the Rome of Vergil and the Greece of Plato.

That is why the welcome accorded to *Iphigénie* is no

unforeseen and isolated accident. The actual classical renaissance in France was preceded and prepared by the renaissance in Provence, just as, in the development of France, the great Græco-Latin awakening of the seventeenth and eighteenth centuries had been patiently prepared by the influence of the southern civilisation, the direct descendant of Latin antiquity.*

There is no event of any importance which has not deep roots in history; for humanity, like nature, never advances by leaps, by caprices. It proceeds by a smooth and slow evolution, in which everything is interconnected and all moves together.

* See Note 11 (at end of volume).

NOTES

NOTES

1. Page xvi.—The name of Rabelais will often be found amongst the greatest and most beneficent masters of all literature. I have, in fact, the utmost admiration for him. Some of my readers, especially lady readers, have reproached me with this cult of Rabelais. They say it is in contradiction with my own ideas. It is clear that they have not understood the main idea of my work !

"But, my dear friend," said a charming lady to me, "how can an 'idealist' writer such as you like Rabelais ? It's a dung-hill !"

"Well, madam, gold shining in the sun on a dunghill is æsthetically very beautiful; and much healthier, even to the sense of smell, than the atmosphere of your salons laden with fashionable perfumes."

"Really, I shall never understand you."

"Dear madam, I must sadly resign myself to that."

2. Page 41.—When these essays appeared in a periodical one of those who rebuked me most severely for my thesis was our dear and great Remy de Gourmont, whose taste for literary discussion, in which he was always a talker and reasoner of the first rank, was appreciated by all who knew him.

One day, when I met him on the Quai Voltaire, looking over old books, he took me to task, very cordially, for the "influence" on the soul of their contemporaries and successors which I attributed to great writers. According to Gourmont at that moment, literature had no influence whatever, either good or bad, and its only importance was in the ability of the writers and the interest of their work. Much to my surprise and joy, I read later, in relation to Chateaubriand, the sentence I have quoted on the title-page of my essay. It is from the *Promenades littéraires* (4e série, p. 249).

I give it in the form of an epigraph, first because it gives me great pleasure to salute once more Remy de Gourmont, who was an original thinker and a marvellous craftsman of the French

language, and, secondly, because I could not find any more
precise formula to confirm my own opinion. If Chateaubriand
did, indeed, lead astray the soul of France, it shows that
literature has an influence, good or bad, on souls and morals:
which was just what I had to show.

3. Page 81.—In support of this statement I quote part of a
letter from Balzac to his sister, written before his marriage with
Countess Hanska:

" Reflect, my dear Laure, that not one of us has ' arrived,' as
people say: that if, instead of being obliged to work in order to
live, I became the husband of one of the most spiritual of women,
a woman of high birth and substantial, though moderate means,
in spite of the wish of this woman to remain alone and have no
sort of relation, even family relation, I should be in a much better
position to be useful to you all. My dear Laure, it is something,
at Paris, to be able to throw open your salon when you like and
bring together people of the best society, who will find there a
pretty woman, as imposing as a queen, of illustrious descent,
connected with the greatest families, refined, cultivated, and
beautiful. That is a fine opportunity for domination."

Who signed this letter ? Balzac or Rastignac ? We might well
make a mistake !

4. Page 90.—Since the time, long ago, when I wrote these pages
on Stendhal, I have come into more direct touch with the man,
in a sense, having lived in the atmosphere in which he spent a
good part of his life, at Rome and, especially, Civitá Vecchia, and
having had the good fortune to make the acquaintance of the
grandson of his great friend, Donato Bucci, who was good enough
to put at my disposal some unpublished manuscripts of Stendhal
and a whole library of books annotated by him. Moreover, I
have tried to reconstruct as far as possible the life of Stendhal in
the little Papal town where he sustained his infinite boredom
with such stoicism, his only support his hope in posterity and
the loyal friendship of the good Bucci.

Certainly I have nothing to change in regard to my opinion of
his work, which I still think demoralising and pernicious, in spite
of—rather, in consequence of—the author's indisputable genius
and the charm which it exhales. But I believe that I have been
too severe and unjust to the man, whom I judged by the misanthropic and paradoxical appearance which he seemed to give
himself in his writings. I intend, therefore, shortly to publish
a work on *The Retirement of Stendhal at Civitá Vecchia.* In this

Notes

I will deal at length with the man on the basis of his unpublished notes, his tastes, his reading, and, especially, the impressions and recollections I have of his almost solitary life.

5. Page 132.—The essay on Musset was written in 1905, when I lived at Naples and contributed to the *Mattino*, the editor of which is one of the masters of Italian prose—Edoardo Scarfoglio. Knowing that I was going to modify my essay on the author of *Nights*, he asked me for a translation of it for a literary supplement to his paper. This supplement was got out by women compositors, mostly young and charming, of dull skin and languorous eyes, who sang poems of Salvatore di Giacomo, set to music by Paolo Tosti or Mario Costa, while they worked.

One evening Scarfoglio received at his office an indignant delegation of these ravishing Neapolitans.

" We refuse to set up this article," they said.

" What article ?" he asked, in astonishment.

" This idiotic article, which abuses love and a great poet of love ! This Frenchman who has written it must certainly be either a fool or a eunuch."

Scarfoglio tried to convince them that they exaggerated, but it was no use. They would not listen. And, laughing, we had to abandon the idea of publishing this scandalous copy.

I recall the anecdote to show the kind of universal popularity enjoyed by men who sing the praises of love, Alfred de Musset above all.

6. Page 139.—I confess that I feel uneasy at times over my strictures on Baudelaire. Of all the poets of the last century he is the one I love most. I read and reread him unceasingly and untiringly. Still, unless I am to abandon all my ideas, I am bound to regard him as a " bad master." His work is certainly discouraging, though it is so moving, and has, in a sense, a spiritualised emotion. As I grow older, I seem to see him more and more separating from the others, Musset, Verlaine, and Stendhal; even from Flaubert, whom the men of my generation used always to couple with him. Baudelaire is deeper, more captivating, more of a *man*. And look at his poetry and the magic of his language ! No doubt it is precisely on that account he has disturbed us so much, and still disturbs us. No one knew as well as he how to stir our souls and enchant our minds.

7. Page 167.—This complete lack of love of humanity, even of a power to understand it, is also referred to in the touching

Life of Tolstoi which Romain Rolland published after the death of the great Russian novelist:

" This permeation of truth by love is the unique merit of the masterpieces which he (Tolstoi) wrote in mid-life, and distinguishes his realism from that of Flaubert. The latter makes a point of not loving his characters. However great he may be in this, he misses the *Fiat lux*. The light of the sun is not enough; we need also the light of the heart. Tolstoi's realism embodies itself in all creatures, and, seeing them with their own eyes, he finds even in the vilest some reason for loving him and making us feel the eternal chain which binds us to all. By means of love he goes to the very roots of life."

It is certain that such a genius as that of Tolstoi would have understood and loved even Bournisien, Pécuchet, and M. Homais himself !

8. Page 211.—In Antoine's lively *Souvenirs du Théâtre Libre*, which has appeared lately, I find the following passage, which confirms what I have written:

" 15 January, 1890. About this time Zola spoke to me about his candidature for the Academy, and said that he was not very confident, in spite of the zeal of Coppée, but that he would insist energetically as long as it was necessary. He sees in the business a continuation of the battle he has fought so long, and an obligation as head of a school."

9. Page 216.—In his *Future of Science* Renan is the first to foresee this inevitable defection on the part of posterity:

" Blessed were the classics, for they came at a time when literary individuality was so strong ! There are speeches in our Parliaments which are as good as the best of Demosthenes, and there are speeches of our lawyers which are comparable to Cicero's invectives; yet Cicero and Demosthenes will continue to be published, admired, and regarded as classics, while the speeches of Guizot, Lamartine, and Chaix-d'Est-Ange will not get beyond the columns of the next day's paper."

10. Page 217.—We must make an exception in favour of the works of Alphonse Daudet; though he was not really a naturalist, or even a realist, in spite of the opinion of his contemporaries (and, perhaps, his own). He died a quarter of a century ago, and is now quite separated from his rivals and imitators. His work, entirely original, is as fresh as when it was first published. Two or three of his books have become classics; while the works of Zola and the Goncourt, especially the latter, are clearly neglected by the new generation.

Notes

11. Page 246.—Compare what Gaston Paris says:

" As we said, the lyrical poetry of the troubadours is historically important. Regarded in itself as a work of art, the impress it received from a particular environment and the artificialities and conventionalities of it have made it, with few exceptions, and in spite of its real qualities, interesting now only to scholars. But at the time of its appearance it attracted general admiration in surrounding countries, and it had imitators everywhere. The artistic poetry of Italy, Portugal, Spain, and Germany was born of it. It is the tree which provided cuttings to be grafted upon and to fertilise these hitherto wild and recently born branches. Its influence was even greater in northern France " (*Historical Sketch of French Literature in the Middle Ages*).

It is indisputable that the French Renaissance of the sixteenth and seventeenth centuries was immediately preceded by the Italian; and the Italian in turn, through Brunetto Latini, Dante, and Petrarch, was profoundly influenced by the genius of the poets of southern France.